JEAN-FRANÇOIS BAZIN

WONDERFUL
BURGUNDY

Translation: Entreprise 35

Photographs

Hervé CHAMPOLLION
is represented by the Top-Rapho Agency, Paris

ÉDITIONS OUEST-FRANCE

The
Priory Church
of La Charité-
sur-Loire.

CONTENTS

A centre, without borders 5

The Burgundy mosaic 11

The first page of the History of France 21

The Romanesque message 31

The flamboyant epoch of the Grand Dukes of the West 45

Burgundy under the monarchy: the cult of the spirit 57

Burgundy in the XIXth century: the great leap forward 67

Modern Burgundy 75

Dijon grew but saved its soul 87

The wine of Burgundy,
the longest reign in history 97

At the heart of taste: the gastronomist's paradise 113

Dates to remember 123

Index 126

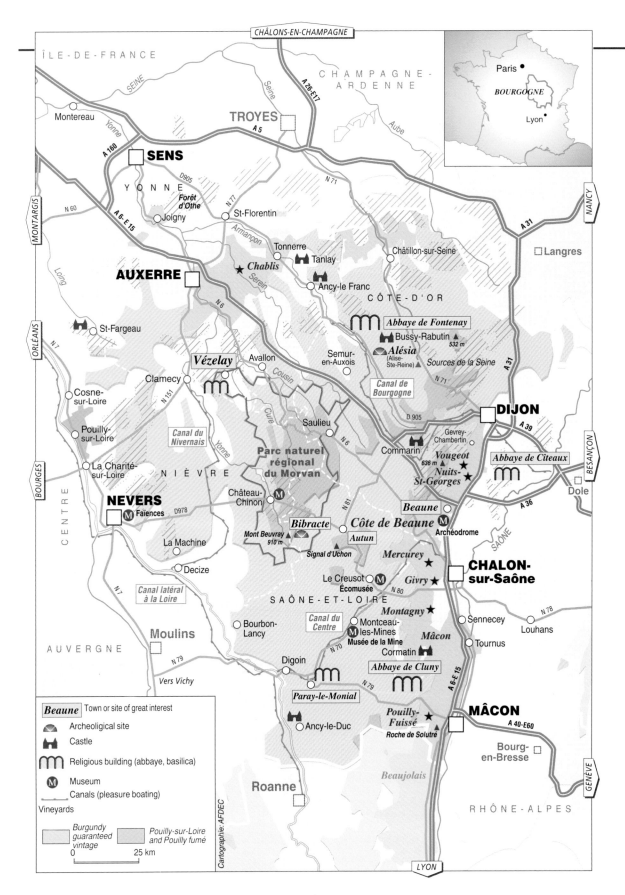

ÎLE-DE-FRANCE

Montereau

SEINE

CHAMPAGNE-
ARDENNE

TROYES

A 5

A 160

SENS

A 6- E 15

MONTARGIS

N 60

YONNE

D905

Forêt
d'Othe

Joigny

N 77

St-Florentin

Armançon

Tonnerre

Tanlay

Châtillon-sur-Seine

N 71

□ Langres

A 31

NANCY

AUXERRE

★ *Chablis*

Serein

Ancy-le-Franc

CÔTE-D'OR

ORLÉANS

N 7

N 6

St-Fargeau

Avallon

Cousin

Semur-
en-Auxois

Abbaye de Fontenay

Bussy-Rabutin ▲

Alésia
(Alise-
Ste-Reine) ▲

532 m

Sources de la Seine

N 71

Vézelay

Clamecy

Cure

*Canal du
Nivernais*

N 151

Cosne-
sur-Loire

Pouilly-
sur-Loire

La Charité-
sur-Loire

NIÈVRE

Yonne

Saulieu

N 6

*Canal de
Bourgogne*

D.905

DIJON

A 39

BESANÇON

Loing

BOURGES

Parc naturel
régional
du Morvan

Château-
Chinon Ⓜ

Gevrey-
Chambertin

Commarin

Vougeot
636 m ▲ ★
*Nuits-
St-Georges* ★

Abbaye de Cîteaux
Ⓜ

Dole ☐

NEVERS
Ⓜ Faïences

D978

La Machine

Decize

Bibracte

Mont Beuvray ▲
910 m

Signal d'Uchon

Autun

N 81

Côte de Beaune

Beaune
Ⓜ
Archéodrome

A 36

SAÔNE

CENTRE

*Canal latéral
à la Loire*

N 7

Le Creusot Ⓜ
Écomusée

SAÔNE-ET-LOIRE

N 80

Mercurey ★

Givry ★

CHALON-
sur-Saône

N 78

Sennecey

Louhans

Bourbon-
Lancy

*Canal du
Centre*

N 70

Montceau-
Ⓜ les-Mines
Musée de la Mine
Cormatin

Montagny ★

Mâcon

Tournus

Moulins

AUVERGNE

N 79

Vers Vichy

Digoin

Abbaye de Cluny
Ⓜ

N 79

A 6- E 15

Paray-le-Monial

*Pouilly-
Fuissé* ★
Roche de Solutré

MÂCON

A 40-E60

Ⓜ Ancy-le-Duc

Bourg-
en-Bresse ☐

Roanne

Beaujolais

GENÈVE

RHÔNE-ALPES

Inset map:
BOURGOGNE
Paris ●
Lyon ●

Legend:

Beaune Town or site of great interest

◭ Archeoligical site

🏰 Castle

⋒ Religious building (abbaye, basilica)

Ⓜ Museum

Canals (pleasure boating)

Vineyards

☐ *Burgundy
guaranteed
vintage*

☐ *Pouilly-sur-Loire
and Pouilly fumé*

0   25 km

Cartographie: AFDEC

A CENTRE, WITHOUT BORDERS

Burgundy, a vital link between the north and south of France,
is a land of encounters and exchanges.
As Jacques Lacarrière says, "The Burgundian is a thousand men in one".

These days Burgundy is one of the twenty-two Regions of metropolitan France.
It comprises the départements of the Côte-d'Or, the Nièvre, the Saône-et-Loire and the Yonne. Nevertheless it has managed to maintain its identity and preserve its own soul. From the depths of time, and nowadays too, Burgundy has always meant something more. It cannot be confined within a simple frame. "Everything Burgundian is naturally universal," wrote Henri Vincenot.

The logotype of the Burgundy Region.
The "B" is inspired by Saint Bernard's signature.
Below: The poster designed for Burgundy
by Bernard Villemot. Photo D.R.

LA BOURGOGNE
UNE TRADITION DE PROGRÈS

CONSEIL RÉGIONAL DE BOURGOGNE

Portrait of Romain Rolland.
Photo D.R.

Fresco in Mâcon
in memory of Alphonse
de Lamartine and his famous
speech of 1847.

The first pages of the History of France were written between Bibracte and Alésia. In the Xth to XIIth centuries, the influence of Cluny and Citeaux spread throughout the whole of the Christian world. In the XIVth and XVth centuries, the Burgundian Dukes de Valois, the Grand Dukes of the West, incarnated the whole of power and culture in Europe at the turn of the Middle-Ages and the Renaissance. With Rameau, Bossuet, Vauban, Buffon, Carnot, Saint-Just, Monge, Greuze, Lamartine, Niepce the inventor of photography, Eiffel, Paul Bert, Marey the forerunner of cinema, Romain Rolland, Vuillard, Colette, Burgundy was omnipresent. Both the sciences and the arts had their role to play.

As a crossing point, if one excludes such secret places as the Morvan, this region, which is deeply marked by social consciousness, is also a land where one can establish roots. Man and the land seem to understand each other so well that sometimes it is difficult to distinguish what belongs to one or the other. History and geography are inseparable here. Since the nights of time men, often from outside, have met each other and settled here, this land of contact and

Old Man Burgundy: Henri Vincenot, author of *The Pope of Snails* and *Disorder*. Photo D.R.

Opposite page: A gateway in Burgundy, opening onto the countryside…

exchange. It is not surprising that one of the classical geographical works (*History of the French countryside*) was written by Gaston Roupnel, from Burgundy. He demonstrates the influence of man over the countryside and the way in which the latter made its mark on man. A marvellous example is the old path which has now become the route for the motorway and the TGV (high-speed train): the road has become part of the landscape. Burgundy is a magnetic land. If the theory of climates needs to be proved, Burgundy can offer the perfect example. Far from the hardships of the mountain and the adventures of the sea, rarely seeing the ground tremble and therefore not fearing the entrails of the earth, Burgundy can set itself up as a model of equilibrium and serenity, calm courage and peaceful ardour: a place which can be trusted in the present world. Its feet on the

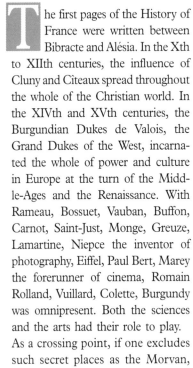

Upper Burgundy, Lower Burgundy

Geographers are still happy to refer to Upper Burgundy (Côte-d'Or and Saône-et-Loire) and Lower Burgundy (Yonne). However, these expressions are no longer in everyday use.

Burgundy's coat of arms

The arms of Burgundy were chosen by Duke Philippe le Hardi (Philip the Bold) in the XIVth century. They symbolically united the blazons of the former Capetian Dukes of Burgundy who had ruled the province for three centuries (gold and azure bendy in six parts bordered with gules) with the arms of the royal family and azure strewn with golden fleurs-de-lys. The Region's logo is taken from this coat of arms. The B represents Saint Bernard's cipher.

Ambulatory of the Abbey Church of Paray-le-Monial.

ground, but nonetheless its head among the stars.

These days it can still contribute a powerful message of spirituality (Taizé, Paray-le-Monial) and several products of excellence of universal renown, whether they be wine, the pleasures of the table, or state-of-the-art technologies such as image and communication, nuclear, steel, special alloys, or transport materials.

Burgundy resembles its image, of course, but at the same time it is very different. Split between the septentrional and mediterranean worlds, it belongs to two cultures. There is no element which links more, said Michelet.

It is one of the vastest regions of France, with 5% of French territo-

ry - bigger than Belgium. But, with only 2.9% of the population of France, it is one of the least populated regions of Europe. These two aspects resume well the whole geography of Burgundy, both physical and natural, human and economic. It represents a considerable area of France but suffers from an exodus of population and a lack of development of the territory. Nonetheless, there are still lands of continuous growth and huge spaces devoted to nature reserves.

As Maurice Chaume wrote, Burgundy has a heart, but no limits. It has good neighbours in six Regions; Ile-de-France, Centre, Auvergne, Rhône-Alpes, Franche-Comté and Champagne-Ardenne, so it is prone to many attractions while benefiting from its own seduction. It is part of the ensemble formed by Alsace, Lorraine, Champagne-Ardenne and the Franche-Comté under the name of the Great East, while still belonging to the Paris Basin (part of the Yonne and the Nièvre) and the Saône and Rhône Basin.

The Prior of Taizé, Roger Schutz, opened the Youth Council in 1974. Photo D.R.

To the north, the plateaux of Burgundy lead to Champagne and the Île de France.

THE BURGUNDY MOSAIC

What splendid nature! Bordered by the Saône, Loire, Yonne and Seine rivers, Burgundy presents ever-changing landscapes, always being renewed, each with its own special personality. From the Morvan to the Bresse region, from the Côte to the Puisaye plains, from the Nivernais to the Othe country...

Burgundy is a mosaic of lands, their roots set firmly in the past: the Gauls, pagi (rural districts) from the early Middle Ages, bailiwicks... Each one has its own character and soul.

The Morvan is common to all four *départements*. The heart and roof of the province, with the Haut-Folin (King's Forest) as its summit at an altitude of 902 metres (3005 ft). As far as the eye can see, 90,000 hectares (225,000 acres) of forest, or nearly a third of the Morvan. This mountain massif has undergone the effects of alpine folding, its periphery is faulted, and a depression due to erosion surrounds it on three sides. The colours of granite blend in well with the grey and blue shades of the slate. The conifers remain green whatever the season and change the landscape. The river Yonne has its source close to Château-Chinon. There are dams to regulate the flow of water: Les Settons, Pannecière, Chaumeçon

etc. In 1970 Burgundy created a Regional Natural Park here (Park headquarters at Saint-Brisson) to protect this vast sanctuary of pure air and wild nature, while still encouraging life to continue.

The Sénonais plain, like the Brie, is a cereal-growing plain. On this side, Burgundy is sister of the Ile-de-France and Champagne. The Othe coun-

Each village (Burgundy numbers 2,044 parishes) lives in the shadow of its bell tower.

Opposite page: The very image of Burgundy, with its roofs of varnished tiles. Photo D.R.

The white splashes of grazing Charolais cattle, born and bred in the fields as families in the pastures.

Roof of the Western World

South of the Auxois region, the landscape suddenly arches its back. This hilly country which may appear unremarkable is nonetheless very high: the Roof of the Western World, whose praises have been sung so often by Henri Vincenot and his characters. Within a diameter of 4 kilometres (2.5 miles), between the villages of Chaudenay-le-Château, Essey and Meilly-sur-Rouvres (to be precise) there is a division between three great water basins: the Armançon and the Serein flow into the Yonne and the Seine; the Ouche descends into the Saône and the Rhône; the Arroux runs to the Loire. This is the water tower of France. The Loire basin (Nièvre, Aron, Arroux, Bourbince etc.) stretches along 4,597 km (2,873 miles) in Burgundy (37% of the water network). The Loire, which is the last natural river in Europe, has been carefully harnessed and its impulsive outbursts disciplined, but this matter is still subject to polemic. The Seine basin (Seine, Yonne etc.) stretches 4,402 km (2,751 miles) here (35%) and the Saône basin 3,512 km (2195 miles), or 28%. The river can rise to very high levels and flood the towns along the Saône from Chalon-sur-Saône to Mâcon. The normal level of the river is 1.5 metres (5 ft). Since 1640, about twenty floods deeper than 6 metres (20 ft) have been registered.

try forms a plateau at 300 metres (1000 ft) altitude, divided up by a series of depressions. This forested clay massif is separated from the Sénonais by the pretty valley of the river Vanne, a tributary of the Yonne. Cider is made here. The Puisaye plain, praised by Colette who was born in Saint-Sauveur, is next to the Gâtinais plain. Sandy soils and clay, with lakes in the middle of the forests, and hedges criss-crossing the countryside: in this region of fields and copses, isolated houses and back roads are lost in the vegetation. Besides fodder crops and cattle breeding, the Puisaye plain has maintained its solid tradition of craftsmanship: stoneware pottery at Saint-Amand. The valleys, or Vaux d'Yonne (Clamecy), lead to the Loire across the country of those two strapping young men, Colas Breugnon and Mon Oncle Benjamin, whose adventures are recounted by Romain Rolland and Claude Tillier.

The Bresse region, with its high roofs, and its free-range poultry...

Morvan lake. Photo D.R.

Right: Châtillon-sur-Seine, Bèze, Laignes; *douix* (resurgent springs) are plentiful here.

Pronounce Auxois as "Aussois" and call the inhabitants of Auxerre "Ausserrois". East of the Morvan stretch the prairie grasslands where the white Charolais and the mottled cattle of the east are bred. Sometimes there is a glimpse of the heavy draw-horses from the Auxois. Formerly this region was the corn belt of Burgundy. Between Auxois and Morvan, Arnay country has kept its personality entire.

Grasses wave in the network of valleys. Stark plateaux tower above. The limestone spurs have served as refuges and look-out posts from the beginning of time (Alésia, Semur-en-Auxois, Châteauneuf-en-Auxois, Thil, Flavigny-sur-Ozerain).

South of the Morvan, the Charolais cattle are raised on the marl of the plateaux and the hills. This rich pasture-land, as in the Brion-

Rural Morvan and the Nièvre are characterized by their many hamlets and isolated farms.

Opposite page: Joigny boasts very beautiful medieval wooden houses.

Right: the belfry of Nuits-Saint-Georges.

nais, is perfect for fattening the white cattle. The race, born from the great Jurassic race, was established first in its Charolais-Brionnais cradle before spreading to the Nivernais in 1773. Since the beginning of the XIXth century, the National Haras at Cluny has developed high-quality breeding of a different nature: horses.

The Dheune (towards the Saône) and the Bourbince (towards the Loire), make up the mining and industrial axis of a depression where a lake existed in the primary era: the Autunois. The filling of the Autun basin is a famous event in geology. The oil shale used to be extracted. As for the autunite, or uranite, this is a fine bright yellow mineral, uranium phosphate and calcium hydroxide.

The hump-backed limestone plateaux extend from the Morvan to the Langres Plateau. This is the famous Burgundy threshold, the ages-old passage between the river Seine and the river Saône, the Vosges and the Morvan.

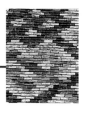

Going westwards, in the Yonne *département*, one comes to the Jovinien region (Joigny), the Auxerrois with its very white limestone (a plateau indented with valleys where the Chablis vines grow); the Tonnerrois near the Langres plateau and still with white stone; the Avallonais which is already part of the Morvan; the Châtillonais where the waters seep down only to emerge later as *douix*, or resurgent springs, like the one in Châtillon-sur-Seine; and finally the Montagne, the country of Henri Vincenot and his books.

Metallurgy was very important in the XVIIIth century, especially in the Châtillonais as well as the Auxois and Nivernais regions, because of the presence of iron ores, wood and water. The technological revolution of the XIXth century left only a few

Burgundy intends
to preserve its balanced nature.
Photo D.R.

Is the Seine a tributary of the Yonne?

At Montereau, the Yonne is wider, deeper and faster-flowing than the Seine. The length of the Yonne is greater than that of the upper Seine. The surface area of the river basin, and the number and size of its tributaries all seem to prove that the Seine really flows into the Yonne and then this river flows through Paris. But, in fact, the Gaulois didn't make a mistake: they had found out that the sources of the Seine… are where they are.

industrial centres which had managed to adapt (Châtillon-sur-Seine and Montbard). The Châtillonais also has several marble quarries.

The regional metropolis of Dijon is at the "very centre" of the Dijonnais region, between the limestone plateaux and the plain of the river Saône. Since the last war, the built-up area of Dijon has expanded greatly, while the lake dug out in 1965 by Canon Kir has modified the landscape and urbanization west of Dijon. To the north-east of the city, the Tille, the Ignon and the Venelle form the land of the three rivers: the Tilles, rich in forests and game, where nature has remained untouched. The Vingeanne is also a world of its own, whose charm is somewhat like that of the Comté at the edges of the Jura and the Haute-Saône.

Did the Côte really deserve the description given it by Stendhal: "a little dry and ugly mountain"? It is

true, though, that he added "are those with wit ever ugly?" This is the last tier of the plateaux of Burgundy, overlooking the vast alluvial plains of the Saône. From here, one can see the Jura and sometimes the Alps. Hard limestone is quarried from its sides (Comblanchien, the French Carrare). But, above all, the vines shape the landscape, giving it its original and attractive character: the Côte de Nuits, the Côte de Beaune and the Côte de Chalon. Wine-growing stretches along a narrow ribbon across the hillside. It hardly extends into the Plain, formerly called the Low-Country. This typical landscape of carefully planted and trimmed rows of vines is, however, fairly recent. Before the outbreak of phylloxera (1880), the vines were grown "in crowds", without any special layout.

The Hautes-Côtes (Upper Slopes) extend across the plateau hugged by the Côte. Formerly, this was called the Arrière-Côte (Back Slope). But the name has quite rightly

Nature preserved

Burgundy possesses 550 protected nature parks. Twenty sites are protected habitats: for example those where the peregrine falcon nests, certain pools and the lower valley of the Doubs. The National Forestry Commission runs four biological reserves (Cîteaux, Is-sur-Tille, Moloy and Lugny). There are two nature reserves: La Truchère-Ratenelle in the Saône-et-Loire with 93 hectares (232 acres) of fossil dunes, peat, pools and woods, and the Bois du Parc in the Yonne with 45 hectares (112 acres) of fossil coralline hills. There are over 1,500 different plants, 155 species of nesting birds and 135 migratory birds, and 50 species of mammals. Of these, 322 are protected species: 147 plants, 120 birds, 26 mammals and 29 reptiles and batrachia.

The wide-mouthed black-bass was introduced into the rivers of Burgundy around the year 1800. The sunfish appeared here towards 1900. The cat-fish, which entered the Paris Museum in 1871 arrived in Burgundy in 1901 via the Bourdon reservoir (Yonne) and spread everywhere. The sheat fish, which has been here for the past thirty years, grows to a fantastic size (over 2 metres long). Woods and copses, alluvial plains, little rivers and pools, peat bogs and marshes, and limestone slopes make up the different natural pockets which give Burgundy its very special character. Among the plant curiosities, one can mention the twisted beeches of Mont Beuvray or Uchon, with their tortured shapes.

Running a comb through the countryside: the rows of vines.

Peaks, douix and lakes

On average, the altitude is no more than several hundred metres. Only the Morvan lifts its head higher, reaching 902 metres (3,006 ft) from Haut-Folin (or Bois-du-Roi) to Saint-Prix (Saône-et-Loire). Most of the rivers have their sources here (the Yonne near Château-Chinon, the Cure in the Anost forest), but there are others in the surroundings of Arnay-le-Duc (the Ouche, the Armançon and the Arroux) and the Seine on the lower plateaux of the Châtillonais. Burgundy can be divided into three river basins, bordered to the west by the Loire which crosses the Saône-et-Loire and borders the Nièvre, to the east by the Saône in the Côte-d'Or and Saône-et-Loire, while the Seine leaves the Côte-d'Or to flow into the Aube (Champagne), letting the Yonne carry on alone in the département. The douix are very special to Burgundy. They are upwellings, Vauclusian resurgent springs where a river which has disappeared into the earth suddenly bursts out again into broad daylight. There are several in the Châtillonais (Laignes, the douix of Châtillon-sur-Seine), but there are other examples (Bèze, Ladoix-Serrigny). Several spas have closed down, but Saint-Honoré-les-Bains (respiratory passages, rheumatism) and Bourbon-Lancy (rheumatism) remain very active. The vast lakes of the Morvan are artificial and fairly recent. The Settons (1858) at Montsauche and Moux controls the flow of the river Cure, ensures navigation on the Yonne and feeds the Nivernais and Burgundy canals. It extends over a thousand acres. At Marigny-l'Eglise and Chastellux-sur-Cure, the Crescent (1933) with a surface area of 420 acres, also controls the level of the Yonne and supplies water to the Avallon region. Near Lormes, lake Chaumeçon (1935) supplies the City of Paris, and extends over 340 acres. Pannecière (1950) to the north of Château-Chinon, with 1,300 acres, also helps control the Yonne while at the same time preserving a minimum level for the Seine and supplying the Nivernais canal. Saint-Agnan (1968) supplies water to the Haut-Morvan and the Terre-Plaine, with a surface of 350 acres. Finally, the Chamboux lake, 190 acres, at Saint-Martin-de-la-Mer near Arnay-le-Duc (1984) provides water for nearly a hundred parishes. There are several projects for other reservoirs in the Yonne.

River tours and sailing are very popular in Burgundy.

been changed to the Hautes-Côtes, which corresponds better with the fight to replant the vineyards, and the traditional fruits which require so much care (blackcurrants, Meuilley strawberries, Arcenant raspberries and gooseberries). Here the Hautes-Côtes de Nuits grow, then the Hautes-Côtes de Beaune, with their own special nuances.

The soils of the Val-de-Saône are covered with alluvium. This favours an agriculture consisting of pastures and arable lands (cereals, beetroot, potatoes). The region of Auxonne is devoted to onion-growing. That of Chalon-sur-Saône to chrysanthemums. The river has long been a means of communication. These days, in Burgundy the Saône acts as the river link for huge barges travelling between the North Sea and the Mediterranean.

In the Mâconnais region, the vineyards appear again, stretching as far as the Beaujolais. The Côtes change their orientation, facing the interior of the country. The landscape is different, and the roof-tiles become Mediterranean. The region around Tournus (the Tournugeois) marks the change-over from North to South, a dividing line. The limestones of the middle Jurassic era

have left traces where, at a single glance, one can spot the spurs of Brancion, Vergisson and Solutré.

Between the Saône and the Revermont (the Jura) extends the region of Bresse of Louhans, famous for its poultry. There was plenty of water in this flat wooded countryside criss-crossed by hedges, and full of forests and pools on clay and sand until the XVIIth century, when it was cleared and inhabited late in history. The houses are very special in character, made of bricks (sometimes with cob walls), overhanging roofs with porches, and Saracen chimneys, for drying sweet corn (panouilles), wells etc.

The Nivernais slopes gently towards the Loire: Amognes, Bazois, the first hills of the neighbouring Bourbonnais (the Bourbonnais Sologne, towards Decize), the vineyards of Pouilly-sur-Loire, Sancerre and Donzy. The pasturelands (livestock fattening) blend in with the forests. This is the most active part of the *département* of the Nièvre, as soon as one comes near the river.

Along the canals, the "still civilisation" described by Henri Vincenot.

The river Saône at Seurre. Near here, Saint-Jean-de-Losne is the leading European port for leisure boating on rivers and canals.

Visits

Autun (Saône-et-Loire): natural history museum. ● Auxerre (Yonne): Paul-Bert nature conservatory. ● Avallon (Yonne): Avallonnais museum. ● Cluny (Saône-et-Loire): haras (stud farm) created in 1806, one of the principal concentrations of stallions in France. ● Dijon (Côte-d'Or): natural history museum. ● Dompierre-les-Ormes (Saône-et-Loire): Pézanin arboretum created by the Vilmorin family at the beginning of the XXth century. ● Montceau-les-Mines (Saône-et-Loire): fossil museum. ● Pierre-de-Bresse (Saône-et-Loire): ecomuseum of Burgundy Bresse. ● Reulle-Vergy (Côte-d'Or): museum of Arts and Traditions of the Hautes-Côtes. ● Semur-en-Auxois (Côte-d'Or): museum with a remarkable fossil collection from the region. ● Seurre (Côte-d'Or): ecomuseum of the Saône.

Natural curiosities

● Bèze (Côte-d'Or): Vauclusian source, resurgent spring: underground caves and rivers. ● Châtillon-sur-Seine (Côte-d'Or): quarries providing marble for many monuments. ● Tonnerre (Yonne): Fosse Dionne, a sacred spring and Vauclusian fountain. ● Uchon (Saône-et-Loire): the heart of the Morvan, in the Arroux valley, the Carnaval granite site (strangely shaped rocks).

THE FIRST PAGE OF THE HISTORY OF FRANCE

*When the whole of Gaul assembled at Mount Beuvray,
and chose Vercingetorix to lead the combat in Alésia, it created a single
and unique nation for the first time. The history of France began then.*

The first page of the history of France was written in Burgundy. It extended over long millenaries, marked by a special prehistoric heritage and numerous sites linked with historic events: Vix, Bibracte, Alésia, the sources of the Seine, etc.

The first traces of the human race appear in Burgundy in the Paleolithic age (from 900,000 to 9,000 years B.C.). Warm and cold periods alternated over hundreds of thousands of years. The mammoth and the steppes elephant populated the glacial periods while the rhinoceros, cave lion and the hippopotamus lived here during the inter-glacial periods. At Soucy near Sens there has been a recent discovery in a gravel pit in the Yonne valley: evidence of humans setting up camp briefly on the banks of a river 300,000 years ago. They had cut up the carcasses of horses, bears, wild oxen and even rhinoceros and elephants.

Man clearly arrived in Europe around the early Quaternary era and was then Pithecanthropus. He gave birth to two great cultures, Abbevillian and then Acheulean, identified by the method of cutting the stone tools he used. Traces of the latter civilisation are found in caves in Burgundy (Azé), on the terraces of the valleys (Loire and Yonne) or in the alluvial lands of the rivers (Saône). In the middle Paleolithic age (from 90,000 to 35,000 years B.C.), warm periods and two cold periods followed each other. The reindeer, mammoth, bison, horse, and woolly rhinoceros fed Neanderthal man. He buried his dead. He lived in the caves of Arcy-sur-Cure, Vergisson, Créancey in Auxois. His civilisation is named Mousterian, much more advanced, and he worked stone and flint with remarkable

The Gauls
are still present.

Opposite page:
The Solutré
rock, dominating
Pouilly-Fuissé.
Twenty thousand
years watch
from these
heights.

Photo D.R..

The Solutrean age

The culture of Solutré is marked by remarkable carved "laurel-leaf" flints (those found at Volgu, Saône-et-Loire, are the finest, in the Chalon-sur-Saône museum). The art was so rich and so original that it gave rise to its own special age in prehistory: Solutrean.
At the foot of the rock of Solutré a burial pit was found, extending over 10 acres and holding the remains of tens of thousands of horses. No-one believes any longer in the romantic image of animals being driven off the top of the cliff to crash down below. In reality, 25,000 years ago, man lived off hunting the immense herds of wild horses roaming between the Clunysois and the Saône plain.

tal and temperate, conifers and deciduous trees grew. The forests were the home of the deer and the wild boar. The hunt was completed by collecting snails and hazel nuts. Agriculture began to appear from about 4,000 B.C., and corn and barley, sheep, pigs and cows fed real villages with big wooden houses (penetration of the Danubians from the north).

skill. The region was more widely inhabited (Nivernais, Sénonais, Mâconnais, etc.) except for the Morvan and Bresse where no traces of human civilisation have been found corresponding to these epochs.

After the early Paleolithic age (35,000 to 9,000 years B.C.) two last cold periods marked the end of the glacial era. Burgundy then became a tundra, grazed by reindeer, bison, the musk ox and the mammoth. When the climate warmed up, the first primitive bull appeared. Cro-Magnon man became a human type close to ourselves. He lived in tents, in caves (Arcy-sur-Cure) or in the open air (Marsangy). His technical skills developed rapidly. He hunted with an assegai launched by a propulsion device. Animals provided everything he needed, including clothes and necklaces. The only decorated grotto in Burgundy is the Horse Grotto at Arcy-sur-Cure. Sculptures of mammoths and deer have been found at Solutré.

The present landscape was formed in the Mesolithic era (from 8,000 to 4,000 years B.C.). As the climate became continen-

Ex-voto in wood to the Goddes Sequana fo at the sourc of the Seine left by a pil grim. Photo D

About 3,600 years B.C. at the beginning of the Neolithic era, a new wave of population arrived in Burgundy from the south, through the Rhône valley. These men brought with them a very sophisticated ceramics industry and an advanced form of culture, and settled mainly in the Chassey camp: they are known as the Chasséens. Then, at the end of the Neolithic age (from 2,500 to 1,800 B.C.), Burgundy became the meeting point of several civilisations. The civilisation of megaliths, which is especially spectacular, extended over the limestone plateaux of Burgundy, with dolmen tombs or chamber tombs under tumuli (Hautes-Côtes de Nuits, for example).

At the end of the Neolithic era (about 1,800 years B.C.) the first copper objects appeared. There was more and more trade with distant lands.

The Bronze Age (from 1,800 to 750 B.C.) finally allowed the Burgundy crossroads to play its full role on the European continent. Trade created wealth (a gold bracelet weighing 1.2 kg (2.6 lbs) was found at La Rochepot, Côte-d'Or). While important ceramics and metallic production developed, a structured human society was gradually set in place, particularly in the Auxerrois

together with the Paris Basin, and also in the Saône valley. Both had very active links with the east: Germany first of all, and then Switzerland and the Alps. Around 700 B.C. the people of the Urn Fields arrived from Central Europe. They incinerated their dead. Their tools, weapons, clothing (discovered by Villethierry in the Yonne) were rich and varied.

The Vix Vase and the diadem of the young woman buried in Châtillonnais country more than 25 centuries ago.
Left photo: Chastel-Courtois.

The mystery of the Lady of Vix

The Iron Age lasted from 750 B.C. to the Roman Conquest (52 B.C.). While the climate became colder and then took on its present character, the First Iron Age, or Hallstatt (from the VIIIth to the Vth centuries before Christ) saw the birth and prosperity of iron-working here. Life was becoming organized. There was a special culture, with huge tumulus cemeteries (Châtillonais) reaching 32 metres (106 ft) in diameter. These were for warriors buried with their swords, often a bronze razor, vessels and vases.

In 1954, at Vix in the Châtillonais, the tomb of a woman of about thirty years old was discovered, lying on a funerary chariot, bedecked and sur-

rounded by precious objects. The Vix vase, a Greek wine-bowl in bronze decorated with Gorgons and warriors is the biggest preserved from Antiquity. It is 1.65 metres (5.5 ft) high, weighs 180 kg (405 lbs), and could hold 1,200 litres of wine mixed with water. No doubt it came from Southern Italy. The gold diadem weighing 480 grams (about 1 lb), and beautifully carved, could have come from the limits of Europe and Asia...

Why was it found in Vix? In the VIth century B.C. Mount Lassois with its oppidum was situated on the "Tin Road" between Cornwall and the Mediterranean world, an obligatory passage between the Seine and Saône valleys. As it was at the centre of two trade routes, the local war-lords probably extorted tolls and became very rich. But why was this young woman, princess or priestess, given such funeral honours? The Vix Vase is in fact similar in all respects to the wine-bowl presented to King Croesus at the same epoch, according to Herodotus. It is evidence of very active links between the Mediterranean, Western Europe, Burgundy and the British Isles twenty-five centuries ago.

From Bibracte to Alésia

The monumental statue of Vercingétorix in Alésia and the remains of the Gallo-Roman city.

In the Second Iron Age, or La Tène (from the Vth century B.C.)

Gallo-Roman bust, 1st century A.D.
at Alise Sainte-Reine, Alésia Museum.
Photo: D.R.

The Eduens, dreaming of taking over Gaul, allied with the Romans and when they were threatened by the Helvetians they called for help in 58 B.C. But winds change, and in 52 B.C. there was a general uprising by the Gauls against the invaders. Vercingetorix, a young prince from the Auvergne, was chosen to become chief of the Gaulish coalition in Bibracte. He retreated to Alésia (Alise-Sainte-Reine) and then was conquered by Julius Caesar who led the siege. This was a significant clash, involving several hundreds of thousands of men. The first page of French history was painful but dignified: the chief of the Gauls surrendered his weapons and, as captive, had to follow Caesar for several years until the triumphal entry into Rome. That very evening, his throat was cut. Caesar spent the following winter at Bibracte and dictated his *Commentaries on the Gallic Wars*. Gaul was dead, but France was born...

The Alésia quarrel

The Alésia quarrel surfaces from time to time: was the siege in Alise-Sainte-Reine (Côte-d'Or) or Guillon (Yonne), Alaise, Salins-les-Bains or La-Chaux-des-Crotenay (Franche-Comté) or Alès in the Gard... Excavations carried out over a century on the Burgundy site as well as aerial archaeology leave no doubt: it took place at Alise-Sainte-Reine.

the region was occupied by several Celtic peoples: the Sénons (Sens), the Lingons (Langres), the Séquanes (Franche-Comté), and the Eduens (Morvan) whose capital Bibracte crowned Mount Beuvray at an altitude of 800 metres (2666 ft). This was a big city of 15 to 20,000 inhabitants spread over 350 acres, similar to the oppida of Central Europe as far as Hungary. There was a single civilisation from one end of Europe to the other. Craftsmanship was highly developed alongside an agricultural rural economy.

Long after the battle, Alésia remains an active city.

The Routes of the Nights of Time

- Alésia (Alise-Sainte-Reine, Côte-d'Or). In 52 B.C. the Gauls united under the command of Vercingetorix held the siege against the Roman armies of Julius Caesar. Several hundreds of thousands of men were under orders, in one of the biggest military clashes of Antiquity. Vercingetorix was conquered, but France was born from Gaul. An important Gallo-Roman city.
- The Burgundy archeodrome (on the A6 motorway at Beaune-Mer-ceuil, Côte-d'Or). It was created at the beginning of the '70s and completely renovated twenty years later, a fascinating vision of a thousand centuries of history in Burgundy. It is the best introduction to the archeology of the region.
- Arcy-sur-Cure (Yonne). These splendid grottoes were inhabited by man 100,000 years ago. Apart from their great beauty, they have left behind them unique prehistoric traces of a certain presence of civilisation, and the only paintings discovered north of the Loire still exist here.
- Autun (Saône-et-Loire). The Romans transferred Bibracte here (Mount Meuvray) and created Augustodunum at the end of the Ist century A.D. This was a huge and beautiful city "sister and rival of Rome", a leading university city in Gaul (ancient theatre, monumental gates, Janus temple etc.).

- Auxerre (Yonne). A Gaulish and then Roman village, marked by the presence of Saint Germain (370-448), an impressive figure of his times and the creator of a sacred Christian centre. There are important archeological collections in the Saint-Germain museum.
- Azé (Saône-et-Loire): grottoes with many prehistoric remains.
- Bibracte: see Mont Beuvray.
- Blanot (Saône-et-Loire): underground chasm.
- Chassey-le-Camp (Saône-et-Loire): important Neolithic site of the "Chasséen" civilisation.
- Chalon-sur-Saône (Saône-et-Loire): the Denon museum contains many archeological items and, in particular, Volgu Paleolithic blades, unique examples of "laurel-leaf" carving.

Autun, sister and rival of Rome, became
a Roman city in the 1st century,
and is protected by monumental gateways.

• Champallement (Nièvre):
Gallo-Roman site of Compierre,
with forum,
theatre and temple.
• Châtillon-sur-Seine (Côte-d'Or):
the museum displays the Vase and the
jewellery of the royal tomb discovered
at Vix, a neighbouring village
(Mont Lassois).
• Dijon (Côte-d'Or):
the archeological museum has
a collection of the ex-votos discovered
near the sources of the Seine
as well as many items of great
archeological interest
(bracelet from Rochepot,
the Blanot treasure, etc.).
• Escolives-Sainte-Camille (Yonne):
archeological site which was
particularly active in the
first two centuries A.D.
• Mont Beuvray (at the Saône-et-Loire
and Nièvre border): a big Celtic
oppidum from the IIIrd century B.C.
then Bibracte, capital of the Eduens.
Apart from the striking beauty of the
site, there are vast archeological
excavations, the archeological basis of
the Celtic civilisation in Europe, and a
museum created by President François
Mitterand, opened in 1996.
• Nuits-Saint-Georges (Côte-d'Or):
the museum gives a picture of the
Gallo-Roman city of the Bolards
(excavations).
• Pierre-Perthuis (Yonne):
Fontaines-Salées (Gallo-Roman thermal
spa, cult enclosure
and Hallstatt wells);
museum at Saint-Père-sous-Vézelay.
• Sens (Yonne): capital of the Senons,
famous in Antiquity for taking Rome in
390 B.C.; this great town was rebuilt by
the Romans and played an important
role in Gallo-Roman civilisation.
There are remarkable archeological
collections in the museum.
• Solutré (Saône-et-Loire):
by the Pouilly-Fuissé vineyards,
a striking prehistoric site with a museum
devoted in particular to the Solutrean
civilisation in Europe.
• Sources of the Seine
(near Saint-Seine-l'Abbaye, Côte-d'Or):
this site, built by Napoleon III belongs
to the City of Paris. A Gaulish and
Gallo-Roman sanctuary where many
wood and stone ex-votos
have been discovered
(Dijon archeological museum), evidence
of the ancient cult of the healing
goddess Sequana.

Statue of the Goddess Sequana, at the sources of the river Seine.

Roman Gaul

Rome had little difficulty in establishing its domination over a land whose ancient customs it respected. These were adapted little by little by the influence of the colonizer. Only the revolt by the Eduen, Sacrovir (21 A.D.), troubled this stability for a moment, but it was quickly repressed. The sanctuary of the Sources of the Seine, with its many ex-votos in wood and stone offered to the divinity of healing (Séquana), demonstrate the persistence of a popular Gaulish culture rooted in the depths of the forests. The Roman camp of Mirebeau is an illustration of a legion's way of life.

At this period the Romans were building communication routes (Lyons to Trèves in particular), substituting Augustodunum (Autun) for Bibracte by choosing a site which was more accessible. Autun became the "sister and rival of Rome". Town planning was based on the Roman model while the villa organized the new agriculture in the countryside. Latin was the language of culture and Autun attracted all the rich young people of Gaul to its schools. The gods were those of the Mediterranean and the East (Mithras, near Nuits-Saint-Georges). After the IInd century A.D. Greek or Syrian immigrants introduced

28

Christianity (the inscription of Pectorios at Autun).

This Roman peace hardly lasted for long. In the IIIrd century, civil wars and Germanic invasions spread trouble and terror. Each large town threatened built a castrum to protect itself. In the IVth century, the influence of Christianity spread. The first saints of Burgundy date from this epoch (Bénigne, Reine, Andoche, Symphorien). There were bishops of Autun, Auxerre, Langres and Sens. This organization, based on the ancient Gaulish nations, was preserved until the Revolution.

Reconstruction of the fortifications of the Alésia battle in the Burgundy Archéodrome (Paris-Lyons motorway, Beaune-Merceuil service area). Photo D.R.
Below: Museum built at Mount Beuvray on the site of Bibracte. Photo Michel Ferchaud.

THE ROMANESQUE MESSAGE

Cluny, Cîteaux, two candles burning in Burgundy to enlighten the whole of Christianity for a thousand years. Together with the spirit of the soul the Romanesque message becomes the essence of beauty.

During Merovingian, Carolingian and Capetian times, which were troubled and bloody, the Burgundian Vision was taking shape. Peoples from the Baltic sea (Bornholm island), the Burgunds, travelled from Poland to Germany, became the heroes of the Nibelungen and the Rheingold, and were pushed further on into Switzerland and Savoie. They settled in the valleys of the Rhône and Saône, and at the end of the Vth century created a kingdom which stretched from Langres to the Mediterranean. Although this did not last, it gave Burgundy its name (Burgundia) and remained marked by civilisation: the wise government of King Gondebaud and his just laws; Clothilde wife of Clovis who led him to be baptised... Then Lotharingia was born, melting into the Germanic empire after the Empire of Charlemagne.

However, Burgundy chose the expression of a universal message, that of Romanesque culture. A thousand years later, the spirit is still the same. It inspires the same wonder. In the Middle Ages, the Church was seen as a bulwark against disorder and misfortune. The bishops played a role which became increasingly important. Some of them, such as Saint Germain d'Auxerre who occupied this seat at the beginning of the Vth century after having commanded the Roman garrisons of the Atlantic Coast, were great civil administrators as well as religious figures.

Christianisation continued, but the old Celtic bases did not disappear from one day to the next, nor even over a century. One knows little about this, but the culture still existed, as seen in the carved stone of the churches depicting, for

The first Cistercian manuscripts (beginning of the XIIth century), in the Municipal Library of Dijon. Photo D.R.

Opposite page:
Saint-Aignan Church at Gevrey-Chambertin: the monks of Cluny kept their most northern vines here.

Cistercian manuscript (beginning of the XIIth century). Photo D.R.

century at Moutiers-Saint-Jean (Côte-d'Or). It adopted Benedictine rule after the Synod of Autun in 670, and its foundations were many and flourishing: Saint-Seine, Bèze, Flavigny, Saint-Bénigne of Dijon, Saint-Marcel of Chalon, Saint-Germain of Auxerre, Saint-Etienne of Nevers, etc.

Cluny at the centre of the world

example, the beliefs and legends of the Gauls.

The saints (Saint Seine succeeding the goddess Séquana, for example) often replaced the ancient local divinities. Then came the times of the monks: the first abbey in Burgundy was founded in the Vth

In 909, Duke William of Aquitaine gave his villa and lands in Cluny in Mâconnais to the monk Bernon and his twelve companions from Baume-les-Messieurs. They founded a monastery there which was independent from any autho-

Cluny Abbey at the height of its splendour. Photo D.R.

rity except that of the Pope. In the space of a few decades and thanks to this autonomy, Cluny became, with Rome, the centre of the Christian world. The great founder abbots were Odon, Aymard and Mayeul who refused the pontifical tiara, Odilon who drew up the famous Truce of God and initiated the commemoration of the faithful departed (The Day of the Dead) just after All Saints Day, Hugues the great temporal and spiritual builder, two others and then Pierre the Venerable who welcomed Pierre Abélard and reconciled him with the Church, and made the first Latin translation of the Koran, etc.

Between France and the Holy Roman Empire, the black monks of Cluny spread their influence across Burgundy, Provence and Aquitaine. They formed a very strong religious militia, with a shoulder-to-shoulder team spirit, as Georges Duby describes it.

England and Castille joined the movement. The political and religious edifice of Western Europe swung to give way to a new conquering rural culture. Cluny followed the Benedictine rule, but adapted it in its own way. Wealth? No-one could put this to the service of God better than the Order itself. Thus, Cluny lived in opulence without any qualms of conscience. There was no great concern about intellectual study or manual work, for everything was a hymn to the glory of the Lord. The church sang the divine offices around the clock. Ceremonies were the apotheosis of Cluny. Thus the unceasing search for beauty, financed by the whole of Christianity and conceived as a homage to God.

Historical heritage:
Cluny preserves precious remains of its architectural glory.

At the height of its glory (XIIIth century) the Order of Cluny included 10,000 monks in a thousand buildings and spread across the greater part of Europe. The monk devoted himself basically to prayer and church services. The liturgy flowered in Cluny in an abbey church which was extended century after century until it became the biggest church of Christendom (Cluny III begun in 1080) until the construction of Saint Peter's in Rome. Callixte II was elected Pope here. The Order disappeared at the time of the

Capitals from the former Cluny Abbey.
From left to right:
Ver primos flores… (Spring rites?); *Tertius Impingit…* (a young man playing a psaltery);
the four rivers of Paradise and the four trees of Paradise (apple tree, fig tree, almond tree and vine).

The Autun Eve, no doubt carved by Gislebert. She picks the apple negligently, as if it didn't matter.

Revolution, and the abbey church was largely destroyed at the beginning of the XIXth century.

Paray-le-Monial, Autun, Tournus, Nevers, La Charité-sur-Loire, Auxerre, Vézelay, Dijon, everywhere Romanesque architecture was singing the praises of God. Around the year one thousand, Burgundy was covered with a white coat of churches, according to the description used by the Burgundian monk Raoul Glaber. The Brionnais illustrated this blossoming to perfection. In 1002, Guillaume de Volpiano started to build the abbey church of Saint-Bénigne in Dijon, and its circular crypt still exists under the present cathedral. This work coincided with the disappearance of the first Duchy of Burgundy, like a flame springing from the cinders. The sculptures of the churches expressed the elevation of the soul and a deep understanding of human nature. As an example, the *Eve of Autun*, a work by Gislebert, one of the rare artists from this era to have left his name behind him.

The Romanesque message was to pass a second time through Burgundy, in just as universal a way but with very different overtones.

The rise of Cîteaux

Reacting against Cluny, its pomp and wealth (whichever way the wind may turn, Cluny will still collect its rents), Saint Robert de Molesme founded the abbey of Notre-Dame de Cîteaux in 1098, on the marshy plain of the Dijonnais Low-Country. This "New Monastery" turned back to the austere life of the old monks, a return to the Saint Benoît rule. In the year 1112, the future Saint Bernard accompanied by twenty young people and members of his family gave a decisive boost to this humble foundation. The white monks took over the Christian world of the XIIIth century, just as Cluny did before. Within a period of only forty years, Cîteaux became head of an Order of 343 abbeys and at the peak of the influence of this spiritual adventure, one could count 762 monasteries, from Scotland to the Holy Land, from Lithuania to Portugal...

Saint Bernard was the dominating figure of his times, the XIIth century. He blamed Cluny, fought ceaselessly against Abélard who, in his eyes, was guilty of "reasoning", criticized Rome, launched crusades, advised kings, refused honours and preached in the South against the Catharians. He made his monks work, as a return to humility.

The Cîteaux message was reflected in the inspired bareness of the stone, an absolute renunciation which can still be seen in Fontenay Abbey. There was no tympanum or capital to distract the regard or thought, or to recount stories or legends. This purity left a deep impression on Christianity. The abbey was closed down under the Revolution and lost part of its buildings. The tomb of Philippe Pot was moved to the Louvre, the manuscripts from the library were sent to Dijon. The Trappists were reinstalled in Cîteax which remained the

Above left: The Saint-Étienne Cathedral at Auxerre.

Cîteaux still has fine old buildings which are being restored for the millenium, library and church law house. Photo D.R.

Sites of inspiration

Cîteaux (Saint-Nicolas-lès-Cîteaux, (Côte-d'Or)
the abbey was founded in 1098, head of the Order of the Trappist Cistercians.

La Boulaye (Saône-et-Loire)
at Plaige, the Temple of a Thousand Buddhas and the Community
of the Buddhist monks of Kagyu-Ling.

La Pierre-qui-Vire (near Quarré-les-Tombes and Saint-Léger-Vauban, Yonne):
the Benedictine abbey was founded in 1850 and publishes the Zodiac collection,
works devoted to universal Romanesque art.

Nevers:
the Saint-Gildard convent and the reliquary of Saint Bernadette de Lourdes.

Paray-le-Monial (Saône-et-Loire)
to the memory of Saint Marguerite-Marie Alacoque and
Saint Claude de la Colombière, the Sacred Heart and the Sessions
of the Emmanuel (Charismatic Renewal) each summer.

Val des Choues (between Essarois
and Villiers-le-Duc, Côte-d'Or):
former head of Order, this old abbey dating
back to the XIIth century offers a site of
great austerity in the Châtillon forest yet
remains very welcoming.

Taizé (Saône-et-Loire)
The Christian ecumenical community
founded by Roger Schutz,
which each year sees countless meetings,
essentially between young people,
and the Reconciliation Church.

masterpiece of 120 monasteries throughout the world. Another branch of the original tree still exists, with the monks of Lérins. Cîteaux abbey is still alive, and its 9th centenary is to be celebrated in 1998.

But the world was changing. The vault on intersecting ribs, typical of Gothic architecture, appeared in 1140 at Vézelay, Sens and Pontigny. The choir of Auxerre cathedral marked this evolution more clearly in 1215. Then came the explosion of Burgundian Gothic art, particularly in Dijon (Notre-Dame), Semur-en-Auxois, Clamecy and in towns or villages like Varzy, Saint-Père-sous-Vézelay or Saint-Seine-l'Abbaye.

Paray-le-Monial Church.

Fresco from the apse of Anzy-le-Duc.
Photo D.R.

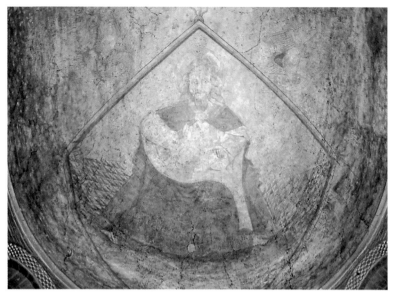

The breath
of the soul

Burgundy is a living pilgrimage. Many figures of Christianity have been added to the founding saints. A nun at the Visitation of Paray-le-Monial, Saint Marguerite-Marie (1647-1690) beheld the revelation of the love of Christ under the form of the Sacred Heart. She is at the origin of this devotion which has become universal. Each year Paray-le-Monial holds sessions of the Charismatic Renewal (Community of the Emmanuel).

From 1866 to her death in 1879, Saint Bernadette of Lourdes lived among the sisters of Nevers. She is buried in the chapel of the Saint-Gildard convent where her body lies in a reliquary.

Saint Catherine Labouré (1806-1876), a nun of the Daughters of Charity in the convent of Rue du Bac in Paris, and who was favoured by appearances of the Virgin (the miraculous Medal) was born in Fain-lès-Moutiers near Montbard.

Elisabeth of the Trinity was a Carmelite nun from Dijon, and Anne-Marie Javouhey, from Chamblanc in the Côte-d'Or, became "the mother of the Black People" thanks to her generous apostolate, especially in Guiana.

The Springtime
of Taizé

Roger Schutz, whose father was a Swiss Protestant pastor and whose mother was from Burgundy, studied theology in Lausanne. In 1940, he decided to create a retreat for silence and work. He visited Cluny, and by chance found a property on sale in Taizé, a neighbouring village. In the autumn of 1944, he and three companions settled here. This community with its ecumenical vocation, accepts Protestant, Anglican and

Fresco from the apse of the Abbey Church of Paray-le-Monial.

Fresco of Berzé-la-Ville.

catholic brothers. In 1949 the Rule was born. And with it, a commitment for life.

The Reconciliation church was erected in 1962. Many young people come to this inspired hill which has become a reference within the Christian church. The prior Roger Schutz built up a major authority. In 1974 he opened the Youth Council whose sessions now take place in all quarters of Europe and the world. The ideas of Taizé are: to practise prayer and contemplation, to look to a better world

Monks of Cîteaux,
900 years later... Photo D.R.

Detail from the western portal
of Semur-en-Brionnais church.

by taking the initiative to help man as victim of man, and to rediscover the unity of faith and hope. Pope Jean XXIII called it a "little Spring". Jean-Paul II visited it.

In La Boulaye near Toulon-sur-Arroux the Temple of a Thousand Buddhas, Kagyu-Ling, has been erected. The community was created in 1974 by the master Kalou Rinpotché and by priests practising Tibetan Buddhism (Bhoutan). The temple was inaugurated in 1987 (Vajrayana Buddhist Centre).

The rosary of Romanesque churches

✎ Anzy-le-Duc (Saône-et-Loire) ✎

An octagonal bell-tower marks one of the most
beautiful churches of the
Brionnais region (XIth century)

✎ Autun (Saône-et-Loire) ✎

Saint-Lazare cathedral built between 1120 and 1130 is one of the
major works of Cluny art. There are
remarkable statues, some of them the work of a sculptor whose
name in known, Gislebert (tympanum, capitals and Eve asleep, in the
Rolin museum).

✎ Auxerre (Yonne) ✎

Striking pre-Romanesque crypts of the Saint-Germain abbey
church containing frescoes from the IXth century painted by the
monk Frédilo; Romanesque crypts (XIth century) in the Saint-Etienne
cathedral rebuilt in the Gothic style.

✎ Avallon (Yonne) ✎

Former Saint-Lazare collegiate church (XIIth century nave,
Xth century crypt, main porches of the façade).

✎ Beaune (Côte-d'Or) ✎

Notre-Dame collegiate church (XIIth century).

✎ Berzé-la-Ville (Saône-et-Loire) ✎

Priory-castle where the abbots of Cluny often lived,
plus a chapel from the beginning of the XIIth century decorated with
Romanesque frescoes influenced by Byzantine art.

✎ Bourbon-Lancy (Saône-et-Loire) ✎

Former priory church of Saint-Nazaire.

✎ Brancion (Saône-et-Loire) ✎

Church in the late Romanesque and Cistercian style.

✎ Chalon-sur-Saône (Saône-et-Loire) ✎

Saint-Vincent cathedral, partly XIIth century.

✎ Chapaize (Saône-et-Loire) ✎

XIth century church with a very high bell-tower.

✎ Châtel-Gérard (Yonne) ✎

Vausse priory built at the end of the XIIth century.
Romanesque cloister.

✎ Châtillon-sur-Seine (Côte-d'Or) ✎

Saint-Vorles church as an example of the meeting between
Carolingian art and early Mediterranean Romanesque art.

✎ Cîteaux (Saint-Nicolas-les-Cîteaux, Côte-d'Or) ✎

Abbey founded in 1098 in the Dijon plain and which remains head
of the Order of Trappist Cistercians. Nothing stands here from the
Romanesque era, but there are two buildings from the XIVth and
XVth centuries and the big building from the XVIIIth.
This sacred place has a soul.

✎ Cluny (Saône-et-Loire) ✎

Abbey founded in 910 in the Grosne valley. Its abbey church, built
between 1088 and 1109, was the biggest building of Christendom
until the construction of Saint Peter's in Rome. A few vestiges remain,
in particular the Holy-water bell-tower; the flour store;
the Saint-Marcel church.

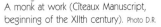

A monk at work (Cîteaux Manuscript,
beginning of the XIIth century). Photo D.R.

⋄ Cosne-sur-Loire (Nièvre) ⋄
Saint-Agnan church (XIth century) Cluny style.

⋄ Dijon (Côte-d'Or) ⋄
The crypt of the Saint-Bénigne cathedral is from the basilica dating back to the beginning of the XIth century; the lower level of a rotunda (a very interesting example of early Romanesque art); the Saint-Philibert church; the cellars of Clairvaux and Saint-Bénigne.

⋄ Donzy-le-Pré (Nièvre) ⋄
Tympanum of a Cluny priory.

⋄ Flavigny-sur-Ozerain (Côte-d'Or) ⋄
remains of the former Saint-Pierre Abbey, from the pre-Romanesque epoch (VIIIth century crypt).

⋄ Fontenay (Marmagne, (Côte-d'Or) ⋄
Former abbey founded in 1118 by Saint Bernard, and wonderfully preserved, offering the purest image of an original Cistercian monastery. Registered as part of Unesco's world heritage.

⋄ Gilly-lès-Cîteaux (Côte-d'Or) ⋄
Former castle of the abbots of Cîteax.

⋄ La Buissière-sur-Ouche (Côte-d'Or) ⋄
former abbey church of the XIIth century in the Cîteaux style. Its construction is described in Henri Vincenot's novel *The Stars of Compostella*.

Above: Chapaize church.
Centre: Anzy-le-Duc bell-tower and the Fontenay cloister.
Below: East end of the Semur-en-Brionnais church and the church at Fontenay.

The angel awakes the Three Kings on one of the Autun capitals. The star lies on their bedside-table. Nothing can be more Burgundian.

One of the pillars of the Vézelay nave.

❧ La Charité-sur-Loire (Nièvre) ❧
Priory and church dependent on Cluny, built in the XIth century and which, despite serious damage, are being restored to their original beauty little by little.

❧ La Ferté (Saint-Ambreuil, Saône-et-Loire) ❧
Remains of the former Cistercian abbey founded in 1113.
The lodgings of the abbey church (XVIIth century) still stand.

❧ Mâcon (Saône-et-Loire) ❧
Narthex and tympanum (XIth and XIIth centuries) of the former Saint-Vincent cathedral.

∽ Montceau-l'Étoile (Saône-et-Loire) ∽
XIIth century church whose main porch illustrates the Ascension and
is one of the finest examples of Brionnais sculpture.

∽ Nevers (Nièvre) ∽
The Saint-Etienne church (XIth century) offers
a perfect example of Romanesque proportions.

∽ Paray-le-Monial (Saône-et-Loire) ∽
The Sacred-Heart basilica was built between the end of the XIth century and the beginning of the XIIth, but it is still not known whether
it was inspired by the abbey church of Cluny or vice versa.

∽ Perrecy-les-Forges (Saône-et-Loire) ∽
XIIth century narthex as introduction to that of Vézelay,
fine bell-tower and sculptures.

∽ Pontigny (Yonne) ∽
Former Cistercian abbey built between 1150 and 1212, at the time
of transition between Romanesque and Gothic architecture.

∽ Saulieu (Côte-d'Or) ∽
Certain parts of the Saint-Andoche basilica are from the XIIth century
church. A wonderful series of capitals.

∽ Semur-en-Brionnais (Saône-et-Loire) ∽
One of the last major edifices of Cluny art in the XIIth century.

∽ Sens (Yonne) ∽
Saint-Savinien church, partly from the XIth century.

∽ Tournus (Saône-et-Loire) ∽
Built in the XIth and XIIth centuries, the Saint-Philibert abbey church
has very original architecture and offers the best example of early
Romanesque art in Burgundy.

∽ Vauluisant (Yonne) ∽
Former Cistercian abbey founded in 1127.

∽ Vézelay (Yonne) ∽
The Saint-Madeleine basilica was built between
1120 and 1140 when the influx of pilgrims required a huge edifice.
This is a masterpiece of Romanesque art, recorded in
Unesco's world heritage, where the architecture,
decoration (tympanum of the Pentecost,
capitals) and the light are in perfect harmony.
There are many rural churches with examples of Romanesque art:
Bois-Sainte-Marie, Bussy-le-Grand, Châtel-Censoir, Curgy,
Fixey near Fixin, Gourdon, Iguerande, Laives, Mars-sur-Allier,
Mazille, Mont-Saint-Vincent, Perrecy-les-Forges, Pontaubert,
Saint-Germain-en-Brionnais, Saint-Julian-de-Jonzy,
Saint-Parize-le-Châtel, Varenne-l'Arconce, etc.

Montceau-l'Étoile.

Jacquemart (Jack-o'-the-clock) on the Notre-Dame church, captured from Courtrai by the Duke of Burgundy and carried as a trophy to his home-town of Dijon. Photo D.R.

THE FLAMBOYANT EPOCH OF THE GRAND DUKES OF THE WEST

Throughout Europe, the XIVth and XVth centuries were the flamboyant illustration of Burgundy's art, a civilisation centred on the Great Dukes of the West. The Order of the Golden Fleece is the purest symbol.

"Grand Burgundy, which had appeared on the horizon of history in a blinding flash, suddenly and irremediably disappeared," writes Joseph Calmette. "But the sparks of impressive success still remain: the boost given to the Low-Countries, for the future; the prestige of a magnificent court; the memory of an active literature and abundant historiography, jealously cultivated. And, finally, the glory of an art which takes its place among the most splendid manifestations of that which honours people and princes the most: taste, aesthetics, human aspiration towards all that is beautiful."

The Dukes' tombs at the Dijon Fine Arts Museum.

"Father, watch out on your left..."

When the young Philippe de Rouvres Duke of Burgundy died of the plague at the age of 19, in 1361, the long line of Burgundian Capetians came to an end. It had lasted for three centuries. There was no direct heir, so the outlook was bleak. Apart from epidemics, there were also the Grandes Compagnies (mercenaries) and warlords ravaging the whole country. The King of France, John the Good, took possession of the Duchy and in 1363 handed it to his son Philip who had earned the name Philip the Bold at the battle of Poitiers. After all, hadn't he valiantly assisted his father by shouting "Father, watch out on your left! Father, watch out on your right!"

First Duke of Burgundy of the House of Valois, Philip the Bold married Margaret of Flanders, one of the richest heiresses in all Europe. When his father-in-law died in 1384 he received the earldom of Burgundy (the present Franche-Comté), Rethel, Nivernais, Artois and Flanders. At that time this constituted a very important economic and trading region. The reign of the House of Valois was to last for a century, and the Duchy reached the height of its territorial, political and cultural influence then.

Above: Charles the Bold. Photo D.R.
Right: Philip the Bold, founder of the line. Photo D.R.

The Dream of a State

John the Fearless succeeded his father in 1404. He tried to dominate France, and had his cousin Louis d'Orleans assassinated, provoking civil war. He was killed on the bridge of Montereau in 1419. His son Philip the Good headed the Duchy from this date until 1467. From his mother, Margaret of Bavaria, he received Hainault, Holland and Zealand, and from his cousin Saint-Pol de Brabant, Limburg and Luxemburg. The power of the Grand Dukes of the West had reached their zenith. Philip the Good allied with the English and fought the Dauphin of France and the Armagnacs. Joan of Arc became their victim. Later, joining the French cause, he obtained Bar-sur-Seine, Auxerre and Mâcon in return. His son Charles the Bold pursued this independent Burgundian policy from 1467 to his death

The Golden Fleece necklace.
Photo D.R.

Top left: Burgundy became French in 1477. Photo D.R.

The roofs of the Hôtel-Dieu in Beaune.

in 1477. He tried to have himself crowned king by the emperor in Trèves, but in vain. He tried to take over Alsace and Lorraine. Defeated by the Swiss at Grandson and Morat, he died in combat close to Nancy.

Between 1364 and 1477, the four Dukes of Valois little by little built up a State fulfilling the ages-old dream of Burgundy. Without any doubt, Philip the Bold, Jean the Fearless, Philip the Good and Charles the Bold were above all attracted by their "far-off lands": the countries of Flanders, Hainault, Brabançon, Luxembourg, where their wealth and economic power originated. By a strange coincidence of history, this Burgundian golden century was part of the chronicle of Bruges, Malines, Ghent and Brussels just as much as that of Beaune or Dijon. For the Dukes, the capital was a "family house". They were born there and buried there. They breathed in the

odours of the hay-loft there, but real life was elsewhere. Luckily, perhaps. While the Dukes pillaged, killed and burned down everything in their way, here they devoted themselves to pious works and patronage. Wasn't an algae in Switzerland, blood-red in colour, called the "Blood of the Burgundians" when it started growing in Lake Morat where the soldiers of Charles the Bold had drowned?

The Burgundian Vision

At the time of the Grand Dukes, from the slopes of the Jura to the polders of Friesland, from the vineyards of Mâcon to the dunes of Helder, from the quays

Moses' Well in Dijon.

it never completely understood. It was amazed and speechless when the Bold - who had spent only one week in Dijon in the whole of his adult life - demanded a kingdom of Burgundy "which the French had usurped long ago". This Lotharingia had existed briefly, but six centuries earlier... Considered thus, the Burgundian Vision, this Middle Kingdom, between France and Germany, was sleeping its last sleep in the church of Notre-Dame in Bruges, enclosed in the mausoleums of the Bold and his daughter Marie. The Franche-Comté belonged to the empire, Burgundy to the kingdom. No-one thought any more about a "Free Burgundy", except for a nazi perversion during the Second World War which remained without echo here. Do not say anything too nice about Louis XI to a Burgundian...

However, from the Burgundian Vision there remained an approach to Europe, frequently recalled by Otto de Hapsburg, parliamentary deputy from Bavaria and descendent of the Grand Dukes. "If Europe is to survive, it will be through the spirit of Burgundy. There is no other way forward". A unit respecting the network of rights, cultures and languages of nations. In fact, and while Louis XI was taking over Burgundy at the time of the death of the Bold, his only daughter Mary of Burgundy tried to defend its rights. She married Maximilian of Austria but died shortly after. The Franche-Comté, Holland and Artois passed into the hands of Maximilian, then Charles V. The inheritance became Austrian and Spanish...

Jacquemart

For six hundred years, Jacquemart has sounded the hours from the roof of Notre-Dame of Dijon. The oldest displaced person in France is not bitter. He was already on the Courtrai belfry when Philip the Bold seized the clock in 1382, and "packed and carted" it to Dijon to punish a rebellion. Since there was no belfry, he and his clock were installed here on the market church. Since then, Jacquemart has been watching everything and ringing the hours following the habits of Flanders.

of the Saône to those of Antwerp, from the mists of the Rhône to those of Zealand, Burgundy was living a dream which sometimes became too much for it, and which

One of the angels of Moses' Well.

The museum of Europe

The Bold left nothing to Dijon, not even the tomb of his father, the first duty of a son. His library is now in Brussels, the Golden Fleece treasure in Vienna, Burgundy's war booty in Bern... Burgundy is split up today, with its family jewels, its silverware, its most precious belongings in the four corners of the world. It is impossible to piece it together without visiting the Historic Arts Museum in Vienna, the Museum of Art and History in Bern, the museums and churches of Belgium, the Louvre Museum in Paris for the tomb of Philippe Pot (an identical reproduction in Châteauneuf-en-Auxois), the museum of Cleveland for several mourners from the tombs of the Dukes, the Walters Art Gallery in Baltimore,

the Philadelphia museum or yet again the Cloisters in New York, the Art Institute of Chicago, etc.

But Burgundy itself is the museum of Europe, since the century of the Golden Fleece illustrates the whole of European culture of the XIVth and XVth centuries. The élite of the arts were attracted here: Claus Sluter came from Haarlem to sculpt the Charterhouse of Champmol, the Saint-Denis of the Dukes of Burgundy, leaving there the Well of the Prophets with a Moses which only Michelangelo himself could represent in such a way with all its interior strength; Claus de Werve, Antoine Le Moiturier, Juan de la Huerta worked on Champmol; Roger Van der Weyden (also called de la Pasture) painted the Last Judgement for the Hôtel-Dieu de Beaune, itself built in Flamboyant Gothic style on the model of the Saint-Jacques Hospital in Valenciennes. The first community was created by a group of nuns from Valenciennes

Moses sculpted by Claus Sluter.

and Saint-Omer wearing the "High Veil", this head-dress in the shape of a cathedral steeple, Flemish devotees, abandoned in 1968. But the sisters are still there, and each year one cuvée of the Hospices de Beaune is dedicated to the Ladies of Flanders. The Sainte-Chapelle of Dijon, the Charterhouse of Champmol, the châteaux of Argilly, Rouvres, Villaines, Montbard (Côte-d'Or) have disappeared or suffered the ravages of time. But in Dijon, the Grand Dukes still live on, through the tombs of the two first dukes or the Well of the Prophets, the Dukes' palace where the look-out tower of Philip the Good still stands plus the kitchens, or in Beaune, Autun, La Rochepot, Châteauneuf-en-Auxois, and Germolles in Saône-et-Loire.

In European choral art, the Flemish-Burgundy School is the one which holds on to the plurality of modal notes with the most tenacity. Maurice Emmanuel demonstra-

The Hôtel-Dieu in Beaune.

ted the relationship between the court music of Burgundy, that of the masters of Cambrai, and the modern works of Monseigneur René Moissenet who restored the choir school of Saint-Bénigne in

Tour of the Grand Dukes

∾ Autun (Saône-et-Loire) ∾
Own of origin of Nicolas Rolin (1376-1461), chancellor of Burgundy. He negotiated alliances between Burgundy, England (treaty of Troyes) and France (treaty of Arras), putting an end to the Hundred Years' war. He built the Hôtel-Dieu at Beaune. In the Rolin museum: the *Nativity by the Master of Moulins* (1480).

∾ Beaune (Côte-d'Or) ∾
Hôtel-Dieu built by Nicolas Rolin (1451) in Flamboyant Gothic, in the Flemish style. The polyptyque of the *Last Judgement*, by Roger de la Pasture (or Van der Weyden) dates to around 1445. The Hôtel of the Dukes of Burgundy (built at the beginning of the XIVth century) is today the Burgundy wine museum.

∾ Châteauneuf-en-Auxois (Côte-d'Or) ∾
Castle and village fortified by the Seneschal of Burgundy, Philippe Pot, which reflects perfectly the epoch of the Dukes of Burgundy. In the church, a Saint John the Baptist is attributed to Claus Sluter. In the castle, a replica of the tomb of Philippe Pot.

∾ Chenôve (Côte-d'Or) ∾
Wine presses of the Dukes of Burgundy (beginning of the XVth century).

∾ Dijon (Côte-d'Or) ∾
The Dukes (in particular Philip the Bold and Philip the Good) renovated the old château and turned it into their palace: the so-called Bar tower (1365), the Dukes' kitchens (1433), the guard-rooms, the tower of Philip the Good or Terrace (1443), the main residential building (around 1450). The former Charterhouse of Champmol (end of the XIVth century) whose doorway and Prophets' Well still exist. The Sainte-Chapelle, seat of the Order of the Golden Fleece, was demolished in 1802 (where the theatre stands). There are numerous works in the Fine Arts Museum: the tombs of Philip the Bold, John, the Fearless and Margaret of Bavaria; reredos by Jacques de Baerze; *Nativity* by Roger Campin, Master of Flémalle; striking primitives and the Chapter-House of the Sainte-Chapelle. Houses from this era: Hôtel Chambellan, Hôtel Morel-Sauvegrain (the nurse of Charles the Bold), Hôtel Thomas Berbisey, the Millière house, etc.

∾ Germolles (Saône-et-Loire) ∾
Château acquired in 1381 and arranged for the leisure of Philippe the Bold. The architect was Drouet de Daumartin, the artist Jean de Beaumetz, and Claus Sluter and Jean de Marville were the sculptors. The Duchess Margaret of Flanders planted vineyards and fruit orchards here, together with cattle raising. Her rose garden was fabulous. The petals were sent to Brussels, to be turned into perfumes.

∾ Nevers (Nièvre) ∾
The first of the "Châteaux of the Loire", begun in 1464 by Jean de Clamecy, Count of Nevers and Nephew of John the Fearless.

∾ La Rochepot (Côte-d'Or) ∾
Château acquired in 1403 by Régnier Pot, chamberlain of Philip the Bold. His son Jacques and his grandson Philippe Pot, counsellor of Charles the Bold continued the building. This eagle's nest was almost entirely rebuilt at the beginning of the XXth century by Colonel Carnot.

∾ Talant (Côte-d'Or) ∾
The Dukes of Burgundy preferred to live in this château on the heights above Dijon rather than in the city centre. It was destroyed in 1598, and nothing remains apart from a fine cellar recently excavated in the hill.

∾ Tonnerre (Yonne) ∾
The entombment of the former Hôpital is evidence of the art of the Claus Sluter workshops for the Champmol Charterhouse.

In Dijon, the Burgundy Governmental Palace built on the former Dukes' Palace (in particular the Terrace tower).

Right: The archangel Saint Michael in the *Last Judgement* in Beaune. Photo D.R.

Below: The weepers (mourners) on the tombs of the Dukes of Burgundy in Dijon. Photo D.R.

Madonna and Child (XVth century), Rolin Museum in Autun.

Dijon in 1895. These days, the school still follows the sacred path, in the same spirit as the voices of the angels of Saint-Chapelle five centuries ago.

Seigneurs of the best wines of Christendom

Was the Burgundian language enriched by Flemish words? One can refer to the *annuette,* a tuberous vetch which both the wild boar and men formerly liked to eat, and whose name comes from the Flemish "earth nuts". You are a real Burgundian! they say in Holland about a gourmet. The wealth of the Burgundy court remains engraved in the memory. The Dukes called themselves the "Seigneurs of the best wines of Christendom".

After many centuries of religious and local consumption, Burgundy wines suddenly appeared on the table. They became part of diplomatic negotiations. They became an instrument of power, a brand image, a business gift. In fact, wine acquires its image of grandeur only when it is backed up by political and economic power. In history, for example, Shiraz, Samos, Falerne. Belgium still remains one of the most faithful clients of Burgundy wines, right from the time of the Dukes. The latter were responsible for its virtues, and the clause of August 6, 1395, is still in force as regards respect for the quality and protection

of the consumer. Le Clos des Marcs d'or in Dijon and the wine presses of Chenôve belonged to the House of the Dukes which owned vineyards and cellars in Beaune, Pommard and Volnay... Gastronomy, the taste for celebrations, the art of banquets, were all a Ducal and Flemish contribution to the Burgundy temperament. These

The Château de Meursault cellars.

days one can still see evidence of this when the Brotherhood of the Knights of Tastevin celebrate their Chapter and the Clos de Vougeot becomes the best guest table of France.

What a wonderful breath of air for Burgundy! This province, living on its own lands and with moderate ambitions suddenly saw its people called to higher tasks. Nicolas Rolin, for example, chancellor of Philip the Good, who founded the Hôtel-Dieu of Beaune. Its lands extended, and its horizons grew. And soon, with monarchic or republican absolutism, it rediscovered the happiness of domestic tranquillity. Sometimes dreams slumber under such a snail-shell.

Detail from the Ducal Palace in Nevers, the first château on the Loire. Photo D.R.

BURGUNDY UNDER THE MONARCHY: THE CULT OF THE SPIRIT

*Under the monarchy, Burgundy enjoyed self-rule,
and devoted itself to progress in sciences and arts: Bossuet, Vauban,
Madame de Sévigné, Buffon... Châteaux sprang up and, in town, official mansions.*

In 1479, the Duchy of Burgundy finally submitted and became French. Tonnerrois had already been French since the Treaty of Arras in 1435, Nivernais since 1463, and Auxerrois since 1476. Until the Franche-Comté was annexed by Louis XIV in 1678, the Saône constituted a border between kingdom and empire. Towns built along the banks of the river, Auxonne for example, were fortified because of the many wars. In 1513, the Swiss arrived at the gates of Dijon. In 1636 the imperial army led by Galas ravaged the Saône and Vingeanne lands despite the heroic defence of Saint-Jean-de-Losne.

And there were other problems, such as the clashes between Catholics and Protestants. Burgundy, wise and moderate, refused the Saint-Barthélemy massacres. It took the side of The League against Henry IV, who nonetheless won the battle of Fontaine-Française in 1595 against the Spanish who had come to help the Leaguers. The whole kingdom rallied behind the King. Burgundy was also fairly prudent at the epoch of the Fronde insurrection, half-heartedly taking up arms against the King. The Protestants had to be alert. The Jansenist movement built up its influence in Burgundy, particularly in the bishopric of Auxerre.

Tanlay Château.

monalty) ran the regional administration. There were also the institutions of the monarchy: the governor, a military and political charge assumed by the Condé princes from 1631 to 1789; and the intendant who was rather like a predecessor to the Prefect of the region.

Burgundy comprised the duchy itself, the Auxerrois, Mâconnais

Bussy-Rabutin château.

Stable institutions

The Burgundian Vision rested again. It was no longer a question of redrawing the map of the world, nor of guiding Europe, but one of maintaining its freedom. Until the Revolution, the province kept its XIVth and XVth century Institutions: with its Parliament fixed in Dijon in 1480 with a judicial and political role, and the Audit Office where The Three Estates met every three years to vote and apply taxes. In between, the elected members (one from the nobility, one from the clergy and one from the com-

which conserved its states, Charolais bought by the Condés in 1684, Bresse, Bugey and the Gex region acquired in 1601. Although Burgundy then stretched to the limits of Geneva, the Tonnerrois whose lords were the Clermont and then the Le Tellier de Louvois families, were linked to Paris. As for the Nivernais, under the Clèves, Gonzague and then Mancini families, it kept its own Audit Office and found itself split between various treasury subdivisions (Moulins, Bourges, Orleans, Paris).

The Classical age

The economic boom saw Burgundy change. In Nevers, the Gonzague family imported the art of faience from Italy. Furnaces and forges used the forests and minerals. This pre-industrial iron-working was accompanied by the beginnings of coal-mining. Le Creusot had a crystal works. But Burgundy still drew the main part of its wealth from the land: the prestige of its wines, the floating of wood from the Morvan carrying loads of logs to Paris, the development of the fattening of livestock in the pastures, the expansion of the Charolais race of cattle, cereals etc. The province was active and its leaders dynamic. They started projects for roads, began creating canals linking the Saône with the Rhine, the Seine and the Loire (1783, the obelisk of the Dijon canal port: the will to "unite the three seas").

Dijon had only 20,000 inhabitants, if that. They lived mainly from administrating the province. A law school was created there. The "good families" were those with patents of nobility (magistrates) and the rich bourgeoisie. This class, rising socially, built houses in town with entrance court and garden, restored old fortresses to make more welcoming châteaux in the classical taste, with vast French-style gardens. Before this, the Renaissance here was much more Burgundian (style Hugues Sambin in Dijon), or Italian inspired.

The first woman to encircle the globe

Although Jeanne Baret was the first woman to go round the world, she is little known. But what an adventure! Born in 1740 in La Commelle (Saône-et-Loire), this fearless woman from Burgundy took part in the 1765 Bougainville expedition. As assistant to the botanist Philibert Commerson, disguised as a boy and in reality his girl-friend, she managed to fool the crew. However, she was recognized as a woman when they landed in Tahiti! The couple disembarked on the Ile Maurice in 1768, and Commerson died there in 1773. Jeanne Baret cared for her natural history collections. She opened a cabaret, married a Frenchman, and then returned to her country of birth where she died in 1807. Two centuries later, in 1996, Claudie André-Dehays was the first Frenchwoman to encircle the globe in Space. Another woman from Burgundy, born in Le Creusot.

Pierre-de-Bresse château
and its topiary as guard of honour.

Bossuet. Photo D.R.

Spreading of the spirit

The spreading of the spirit, which was considerable at this time, was to the advantage of the Jesuits who founded colleges in almost all the towns. Saint Jeanne de Chantal instituted the Order of the Visitation. Jacques-Bénigne Bossuet, also born in Dijon, studied in the town. The revelation of the Sacred Heart appeared to Saint Marguerite-Marie in her convent in Paray-le-Monial. The Dijon Academy (1740) played a very active role in all this. It "discovered" an unknown author: Jean-Jacques Rousseau, laureate for his *Study of the progress of science and arts.* Local names include Georges Leclerc, the Count of Buffon, the president de Brosses, Jean-Philippe Rameau. As a monk in Beaune, Edme Mariotte discovered the chemical law which is named after him. Sébastien Leprestre de Vauban was born in Morvan and rethought the science of fortifications. The architect Germain Soufflot left Irancy to build Saint-Geneviève in Paris (The Pantheon). Jean-Baptiste Greuze, who came from Tournus, was one of the most outstanding painters and sketchers of the XVIIIth century. The states of Burgundy founded an arts and sculpture academy which soon became international. They created the Rome Prize whose laureates (Bénigne Gagnereaux, Pierre-Paul Prud'hon, etc.) were evidently well chosen.

Dijon has about a hundred private mansions built in the XVIIth and XVIIIth centuries by the members of the Burgundy Parliament and titulars of public offices in the Province. Photo Jean-Pierre Coqueau.

The time of the *art de vivre*

Most of these dwellings were rebuilt over the years, reconstructed, and redesigned. Although their function was security until the XVIth century, in the XVIIIth century this was replaced by social prestige and *art de vivre*. The "U-shape" was developed, and the fortifications disappeared. The top nobility was not yet at the court of Versailles and often lived "on its lands" (Commarin; Savigny-lès-Beaune, Menou, Chaumont (La Guiche), Cormatin, Montjeu, Montcoy, Pierre-de-Bresse, La Loyère, etc.).

Abbots from monasteries (Clos de Vougeot and Gilly for Cîteaux, La Ferté, etc.) and bishops (Urzy near Nevers) also built themselves castles. Exile in the provinces for figures in disgrace (the Grande Demoiselle at Saint-Fargeau, Bussy-Rabutin at Bussy-le-Grand) enriched the local heritage, for they had to be looked after during the whole of the year... The XVIIth and XVIIIth centuries saw the blossoming of classicism.

Grancey was designed as a little Versailles, Beaumont-sur-Vingeanne, an urban house in the middle of the countryside. The châteaux of Talmay, Commarin, Fontaine-Française, Vantoux, Lux, Digoine in Palinges, Terrans etc. figure among the most interesting of this epoch. There are few neo-classical edifices (Arcelot). The château of Pommard (1800) was influenced by the Italian style.

Neo-gothic appeared (Chastellux, La Rochepot entirely rebuilt in the XXth century). Lamartine took his inspiration from Walter Scott to arrange Saint-Point.

In 1900 Stephen Liégeard offered the wine slopes a Loire château modelled on Azay-le-Rideau (Brochon). This is the last of the thousand châteaux built in a thousand years, if one does not take into account the Poncey-sur-l'Ignon manor built by Charles Huard in the middle of the XXth century, where Roland Dorgelès wrote his last books.

Mont-Saint-Jean.

Époisses.

Ancy-le-Franc.

Semur-en Brionnais.

A thousand years and a thousand castles

The castle era lasted for a thousand years.
In Burgundy there are still a good thousand
buildings like this which testify to the history
of this land. Many were born or renovated
under the Monarchy.

After the fortified enclosures,
the first castles appeared in
the IXth and Xth centuries.
These were fortresses built at strategic
points and acting as residences for those
in power (Vergy, Châtillon-sur-Seine,
Mont-Saint-Jean, Couches, Berzé, Beaujeu,
Brancion, Montréal, etc.).
These strong enclosures could offer shelter
to the local people during wars or invasions
(Grignon, Frôlois, Rochefort, Thil,
Dyo, Joigny, Toucy,
Saint-Fargeau, etc.). Sometimes a city was
created after the castle (Montbard,
Semur-en-Brionnais, Charolles etc.).

In the XIth and XIIth centuries,
the "new castles" were often built
in a high position as a defence
(Châteauneuf-en-Auxois, Chaudenay,
Malain, Igornay, Bazoches,
Druyes-les-Belles-Fontaines, Vallery, etc.).

In the XIIIth and XIVth centuries,
not only the grand lords but also
the lowest ranking knights built
themselves "fortified houses",
or manors protected by towers and keeps.
Cluny fortified a cellar to protect its wine
(Gevrey-Chambertin). Gradually,
these castles became square or rectangular
(La Rochepot, Montigny-Montfort, etc.).
From the XIVth century and particularly in
the XVth, the best military architecture produced
castles where comfort was in no way neglected
(Rozières, Châtillon-en-Bazois, Chevenon,
Germolles, Pierreclos, Arcy-sur-Cure, etc.).
Vauban settled in Bazoches.
The quality of decoration became more and
more perfected thanks to the influence of the
Loire and the Ile-de-France,
in particular in Nivernais and North Burgundy
(Chailly-sur-Armançon, Epoisses,
Fleurigny, etc.).
Architecture was Italian inspired,
with its castles of great pomp (Sully,
Ancy-le-Franc, Tanlay) or
of individual design (Maulne).

Gardens and parks

৵ *Historic gardens* ৵

Middle Ages: former monastic or religious enclosures at Fontenay (Côte-d'Or), Nevers (Nièvre), Bourbon-Lancy (Saône-et-Loire), Courgenay (Yonne - former Abbey of Vauluisant), Val des Choues (Villiers-le-Duc, Côte-d'Or), the former Abbey of La Bussière-sur-Ouche (Côte-d'Or) or the gardens close to the Hôtels-Dieu in Arnay-le-Duc (Côte-d'Or), Tonnerre (Yonne). Châteaux: Chaudenay-le-Château at the Australian painter's Kevin Pearsch (Côte-d'Or); Epoisses (Côte-d'Or); Berzé-le-Chatel (Saône-et-Loire).

Renaissance: Ancy-le-Franc and Tanlay (Yonne); Bussy-Rabutin (Côte-d'Or).

Classical era: Arcelot, Barbirey-sur-Ouche, Fontaine-Française, Gilly-les-Cîteaux (Côte-d'Or); Châtillon-en-Bazois, Menou (Nièvre); Chaumont, Cormatin, Pierre-de-Bresse, Sully (Saône-et-Loire); Saint-Fargeau, Nailly, Thorigny-sur-Oreuse, Vallery (Yonne).

৵ *Botanical gardens and arboretum* ৵

Pézanin Arboretum (Dompierre-les-Ormes, Saône-et-Loire).
Arquebuse botanical garden in Dijon (Côte-d'Or).
Herbularium of Saint-Brison (Nièvre).
Geobotanical garden at Chalon-sur-Saône (Saône-et-Loire).
Park of the Paul-Bert House in Auxerre (Yonne).
Greenhouses of Sens (Yonne).

৵ *Town parks and gardens* ৵

Beaune (Côte-d'Or): Bouzaize park, the squares of the Ramparts.
Chalon-sur-Saône (Saône-et-Loire): rose-garden and Saint-Nicolas park.
Clamecy (Nièvre): Vauvert park.
Dijon (Côte-d'Or): Colombière park (XVIIIth and XIXth centuries) Carrières-Bacquin park (XXth century), the Darcy garden (XIXth century).
Le Creusot (Saône-et-Loire): park of the Château de la Verrerie.
Montbard (Côte-d'Or): Buffon park.
Paray-le-Monial (Saône-et-Loire): Liron park.
Saint-Honoré-les-Bains (Nièvre): park of the Thermes.
Sens (Yonne): Moulin-à-Tan park.

৵ *In the vineyards* ৵

The garden of the Chandon de Briailles Domaine at Savigny-les-Beaune (Côte-d'Or), those of the Clos de Lambrays Domaine at Morey-Saint-Denis (Côte-d'Or) and the Clos-Arlot Domaine at Premeaux-Prissey (Côte-d'Or).

Châteauneuf-en-Auxois. Photo D.R.

Berzé-le-Châtel.

Commarin.

Saint-Fargeau.

Saint-Point Château where Lamartine lived.

BURGUNDY IN THE XIXTH CENTURY: THE GREAT LEAP FORWARD

Gustave Eiffel was born, grew up, and studied in Dijon, before building his 300 metre-high tower in Paris. The Schneider factories in Le Creusot became the melting pot of industrial engineering. The century of the great leap forward.

The winter of 1789 was particularly hard There was not enough corn or bread. The grape harvest looked poor. Riots were already breaking out. The convocation of the States General to Versailles opened the way for expressions of discontent. Complaints books demonstrated the desire for political change (the lawyers showed themselves to be very active in the patriotic movement) and the more basic problems of the rural areas. The majority of the members of parliament from the clergy and commonalty elected in Burgundy joined the side with new ideas.

When the situation became agitated (town municipalities replaced by committees, the Great Fear in the Mâconnais where the peasants attacked several châteaux and were severely put down at Hurigny), the province of Burgundy was split to form *départements* (1791). The former government of Nivernais became the Nièvre. The Côte-d'Or and Saône-et-Loire corresponded to the former treasury subdivision. Avallonnais and Auxerrois were grouped together with the lands of Champagne, Ile-de-France and Orléanais to form the Yonne.

Opposite page:
Modern Burgundy, born in the XIXth century.
Left to right and top to bottom:
Stainless steel at Gueugnon;
Atomic Energy Centre of Valduc;
Alloys at Imphy;
Acrodur at Longvic. Photos D.R.

At the beginning of the XXth century, cattle fair at Autun. Photo D.R.

67

Bresse, which had been Burgundian, was split into three parts, in Saône-et-Loire, the Jura and the Ain. Auxerre became the capital town of the Yonne, but the bishopric remained at Sens. In Saône-et-Loire, Mâcon was the capital, Autun kept its bishop while Chalon-sur-Saône was given the Law Courts. All this reorganization took no more than a few months. But it was there to stay.

From the Revolution to the Empire

Although clubs and societies were fairly active here, Burgundy came through the Revo-

lution relatively calmly. Belief in the Catholic faith remained alive, especially in the Charolais and Brionnais regions, while the majority of Burgundian priests refused to swear the oath of allegiance to the civil constitution of the clergy. Talleyrand, briefly bishop of Autun, soon went back to Paris to start his outstanding political career. The most violent tensions arose when Fouché visited the Nièvre or energetic "special envoys" arrived. But the Terror seems to have been fairly moderate here. Nonetheless, Burgundians were not lacking at the centre of the Revolution. Some, like Saint-Just, Basire or Chaumette were carried away by the torrent of history. Others, like Carnot, Monge, Prieur de la Côte-d'Or, or Guyton de Morveau played a different role: organizing

Cluny Abbey:
The destruction
of the sanctuary
(about 1810-1820).
The marble columns
topped by capitals
are still in place.
Above the great arcades,
the fluted pilasters
harmonize the wall.
Watercolour, Rambuteau Coll.

the armies, creating the Ecole Polytechnique, founding the new order.

During these years and until the beginning of the XIXth century, there was a complete absence of respect for the heritage, and endless destruction due more to vandalism than revolutionary faith. Cluny Abbey, Cîteaux Abbey, the Charterhouse of Champmol, and countless monasteries were knocked down into piles of stones, systematically destroyed while their treasures (sculptures, paintings, libraries) simply disappeared.

Bonaparte was almost a native of the land. He studied at Autun and then as a young lieutenant he lived in Auxonne. The coup-d'état of the 18-Brumaire was greeted with satisfaction. Everyone wanted to see a return to order, and a certain prosperity was built up again. While the first Prefects were organizing the new life of Burgundy, war broke out again. Davout, Junot and Marmont stood out as great military figures from Burgundy under the Empire, while Monge and Denon took part in the campaign in Egypt and contributed to the blossoming of the sciences.

After 1811, famine reared its head again. The great iron-works of Saône-et-Loire and the Nièvre fell into decline, with competition from new processes (coke smelting). Burgundy suffered from the invasions of 1814 and 1815.

The Emperor of Austria installed himself in Dijon; the allied sovereigns met at Châtillon-sur-Seine to try to decide the future of France. The misfortunes of this military occupation and the "blue fibre" (the conquests of 1789, associated with those of the Empire) explain the triumphant welcome given to Napoleon during the Hundred-Days.

Lazare Carnot, born in Nolay in 1753 was not only the Planner of Victory in 1793-1795. He laid down law on job security and opened the way to modern geometry with Gaspard Monge, himself born in Beaune in 1746, and creator of descriptive geometry. All the mathematicians of the XIXth century were his followers. He devoted himself to the Ecole Polytechnique where another Burgundian was teaching, Louis-Bernard Guyton de Morveau, born in Dijon in 1737, author of the first chemical nomenclature, inventor of the disinfection of air by hydrochloric acid and who made the first aerostatic experiment in Burgundy, on April 25 1784, from Dijon to Auxonne: the first journey in a free balloon in the sky.

This was when Burgundy dug its canals.

Heavy industry

From 1815 to 1914, Burgundy saw a series of changes. Politically, it went underground and suffered in silence continuing to interest geographers, historians and artists. Three-quarters of the population lived in rural areas, divided between three worlds: vines, much more extensive than today, fairly prosperous with forward-looking ideas; wooded areas (nearly the whole of the Nièvre and the Puisaye, the Morvan, the west of Saône-et-Loire) and open fields (the vast cultivated expanses of the Châtillonais, the plateaux, and most of the Yonne).

Heavy industry was introduced by the Marmont family at Sainte-Colombe (Châtillonais), the Boignes at Imphy and Fourchambault (Nivernais), and above all the Schneider family which came to Le Creusot in 1836. This soon became the most powerful metallurgical plant in France, producing locomotives and cannons for the whole world. The Chagot family exploited the coal-mines of the Blanzy basin and Epinac. The old iron works gave way to modern forges and furnaces. By their thousands, the sons of peasants became factory workers, in semi-rural, semi-urban surroundings, in a system which offered a relatively decent living for the whole of their life (a job, lodging, studies and social promotion, medical care and retirement pension) as soon as they integrated into a totally hierarchical society organized from the top.

Up until the IIIrd Republic, the traditional notability (the society of the Old Regime reinstalled at the time of the Empire, the new owning classes) ran life in Burgundy alongside the young industrial dynasties. The road system was improved and one could finally cross the Morvan from Nevers to Dijon. The Centre canal, finished in 1793 was completed by the canals of Burgundy (1832), and the Rhône-Rhine (1834), the canal lateral to the Loire (1838) and the Nivernais canal (1842). The railway was to arrive shortly: the Paris-Lyons-Marseilles via Dijon went into service in the middle of the century, while Nevers was on a branch line (1851) on the Paris-Clermont-Ferrand route.

Politically, Burgundy tended towards liberalism, doubtless linked to the interests of the notability, while still refusing to be ultra-royalist. The Napoleonic tendency kept its influence. Thus the vete-

Nicéphore Niepce
The first photo

"I set the apparatus in the room where I worked, in front of the birdcage with the casement windows wide open. I carried out the experiment using the procedure you know so well, dear friend, and I saw, on the white paper, all of the birdcage which could be seen from the window and a pale image of the casement windows which were less illuminated than the external objects. I could see the effects of the light on the image of the birdcage, right up to the window-frame..." Nicéphore Niepce, in this letter to his brother (May 5, 1816), describes what he called a very imperfect trial. However, it was one the greatest inventions of modern times: photography. It was in Saint-Loup-de-Varennes near Chalon-sur-Saône.
He continued to reproduce this "representation of nature" over ten years. There is still an image (from about 1826) preserved in Austin (Texas) in the Gernsheim collection.

Burgundy is the Valley of the Image. Between Dijon and Lyons, there were successive inventions: photography, reproduction on paper of photography on plate glass (Abel Niepce de Saint-Victor), chronophotography (invented by Etienne-Jules Marey from Beaune) which led to the cinema of the Lumière brothers, then the electronic camera (André Lallemand) and the first zoom, the pancinor (Roger Cuvillier).

La Vallée de l'image®
est en Bourgogne

70

ran Claude Noisot asked François Rude to make a sculpture of Napoleon awakening to immortality for his property at Fixin. The revolutionary July days (1830) were greeted with favour. The progressive movement also advanced, with the support of Alphonse de Lamartine, the great poet from Burgundy who was actively involved in the battle of ideas. Although the conservatives held on to most of the reins of power, the evolution of the spirit due to the development of learning became more and more evident.

Under the Second Empire, expansion was marked. Napoleon III gave a boost to the economy through an open policy to the surrounding world. Burgundy even sold its locomotives to England! Trade union opinion began to appear; the times were changing. Republican ideas came forward. But there were other upheavals on the horizon, like the growing attraction of Paris which emptied

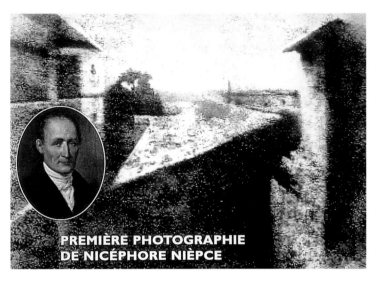

PREMIÈRE PHOTOGRAPHIE DE NICÉPHORE NIÈPCE

The first photograph by Nicéphore Nièpce.

the Morvan, and even the lure of Lyons to some extent from the south, the slowing down of the industrial basins of Northern Burgundy, the railway taking over the canals etc. A distant heir of Jacobism, an extreme leftist tendency reared its head when Napoleon III took power in 1851 (Republican uprising of Clamecy, put down swiftly). It was to remain

Étienne-Jules Marey, cinema pioneer.

ÉTIENNE-JULES MAREY, PIONNIER DU CINÉMA

Gustave Eiffel. Photo D.R.

alive in Burgundy. The Franco-German war of 1870 raised emotions: invasion, the presence of Republicans organizing the resistance, the support from Garibaldi and his "redshirts" which already looked like international brigades. Despite a few weaknesses in the Nièvre, the Republican party firmly established itself under the IIIrd Republic: Paul Bert in Auxerre; Sadi Carnot, Eugène Spuller and Joseph Magnin in Côte-d'Or.

Even though Burgundy was not reluctant to join radical France, which was to last for a long period, what a time of changes! These included the appearance of electricity, the telephone; Gustave Eiffel (born in Dijon in 1832) who built the 300 metre (1,000 ft) tower in Paris which bears his name, Paul Bert (born in Auxerre in 1833) who created modern physiology; Louis Cailletet (born in Châtillon-sur-Seine in 1832) who was the first to liquefy atmospheric air and became the father of liquid air; Bernard Courtois (born in Dijon in 1777) who discovered iodine; Jean-Joseph Fourier (born in Auxerre in 1768) who invented mathematical physics; Hippolyte Fontaine (born in Dijon in 1833) who was the first to demonstrate that one could carry electricity from one point to another, and Pierre Larousse (born in Toucy in 1817) who wrote a whole dictionary about it all.

Visits

⌘ Chalon-sur-Saône (Saône-et-Loire) ⌘
The Niepce museum, dedicated to the history of photography invented in Burgundy by Nicéphore Niepce.

⌘ Fixin (Côte-d'Or) ⌘
Monument by François Rude depicting the *Awakening of Napoleon*.

⌘ La Machine (Nièvre) ⌘
In memory of the mine, which closed down in 1974 (museum).

⌘ Le Creusot (Saône-et-Loire) ⌘
Ecomuseum and the museum of the François-Bourdon Academy, in the former Schneider château (La Verrerie).

⌘ Montceau-les-Mines (Saône-et-Loire) ⌘
Open-cast mining continues. The last pits closed between 1980 and 1990. Mine museum at Blanzy.

⌘ Lamartine country (Saône-et-Loire) ⌘
Around Mâcon, the château de Monceau, Milly, Bussières, the château de Pierre-Clos and that of Saint-Point, to follow the steps of the great poet and major political spirit of the XIXth century.

⌘ Sully (Saône-et-Loire) ⌘
The château where Edme-Patrice de Mac-Mahon was born in 1808, the future duke of Magenta, Marshal of France and first President of the IIIrd Republic.

Coal and steel

The mining and industrial ensemble of Le Creusot-Montceau was split up at the beginning of the XIXth century. For a century, the Chagot family ruled over the Blanzy coal basin (30,000 tons extracted in 1833, 1 million tons around 1900) while the Schneider family settled in Le Creusot. Loved or hated, the mine always holds a fascination: social conflicts like the "Black band" (the strike of 1901 which lasted 108 days), great tragedies (89 deaths in 1867 and another 21 in 1895 at the Five-sous pits, the danger money paid to the workers, and the pits renamed Sainte-Eugénie under the Second Empire), Italian and then Polish immigration etc. The town of Montceau-les-Mines was only built in 1856, by dismembering adjacent communes.

The power hammer of Le Creusot, able to crack the skin of a walnut without squashing the flesh, made a great impression on the heroes of the *Tour of France by two children* a century ago. Symbol of the industrial genius of the city, this 21 metre (70 ft) high machine with its 100-ton power weight (1876-1924) now stands in one of the city squares. In its time, it could forge enormous steel parts. The first coke smelting in France took place in Le Creusot (1785). The former crystal works was transferred to Baccarat and became a cannon foundry. With their metallic constructions of bridges, lighthouses, armour plating, ships, weapons and cannons, locomotives, the Schneiders made Le Creusot the French iron and steel capital in the 1840's.

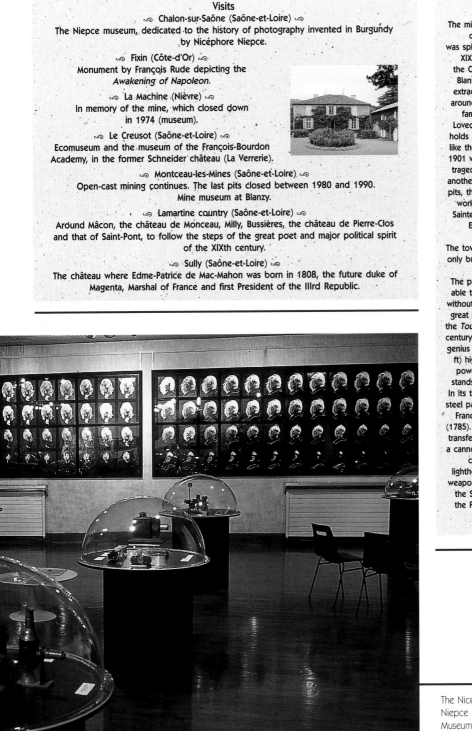

The Nicéphore-Niepce Museum, Chalon-sur-Saône.

MODERN BURGUNDY

The vines hide a wealth of economic and technological progress.
Burgundy is also Photo Valley, the Pinnacle of Taste,
Europe's Inland Port, Four hands at work.

Burgundy today is one of the most visited regions of France thanks to its tourist image. The arts and pleasures of life meet here with prestigious museums, the cradle of Romanesque art, over a thousand kilometres of rivers and canals for pleasure boating, and landscapes which are attractive and always changing.

When it is not devoting itself to welcoming its visitors, Burgundy is developing countless different activities. It does not simply hide behind a vine-leaf!

The Burgundian awakening

After several successive reforms, under the Vth Republic Burgundy became a Region. The first trials at regionalisation had involved Bur-

gundy and the Franche-Comté. This marriage was difficult, and four close départements had to be brought in (Côte-d'Or, Nièvre, Saône-et-Loire and Yonne) to satisfy the Burgundian Vision.

However, there is no waiting for the end of the XXth century before waking up.

In the early '30s one could wonder what miracle was needed to extract the Burgundy wine-gro-

Opposite page:
The T.G.V. (high-speed train) has crossed Burgundy from one end to the other since 1981. Photo D.R..

Thomson Multimédia in Auxonne: digital television decoders. Photo D.R.

The Dijon Bareuzai: wine-grower trampling his grapes.
Photo D.R.

wer from his crisis, and from a deep economic lethargy. And then came the reaction: an incredible influx of new oxygen, a tumult of new ideas which half a century later had changed the situation completely. Burgundy did not give up. Around Jacques Copeau, founder of the New Literary Review and the Vieux Colombier Theatre in Paris, and theatre renovator, a happy band of young actors set themselves up in Pernand-Vergelesses: the *Copiaux* (Marie-Hélène and Jean Dasté etc.). The Belgian writer Maurice des Ombiaux wrote a book about the Burgundy Genius. Colette kept her Burgundy accent in the capital. Gaston Roupnel passionately praised Burgundy while still continuing his geographical work. Gaston Gérard founded the Dijon Gastronomy Fair and became representative of tourist Burgundy. Maurice Perrin de Puycousin created the first two museums of local art and traditions at Tournus and Dijon. In 1932 Count Jules Lafon launched the Paulée de Meursault and its literary prize. The Mâconnais Georges Rozet soon thought up the Trois Glorieuses (three days of charity wine auctions) around the Wine Auction of the Hospices de Beau-

ne, honoured again. After 1934, in Nuits-Saint-Georges, came the Tastevin, the Turning Saint-Vincent, and the Tastevinage.

To be brief, Burgundy which had simply been crossed out by the revolutionaries was reborn in splendour. It went beyond the *départements,* inspired and then integrated new ardours, based on the land and assembling the population. One suddenly realised that the word Burgundy was worth gold. Paris took a long time to understand.

From one war to the next

Burgundy did not suffer the ravages of the First World War on its own soil, but after the conflict each commune built a monument in memory to its dead. One man in ten, and sometimes more, interminable lists of soldiers mowed down at Verdun, the Champ des Dames. Every single family was touched. Burgundy was already beginning to lose its population, and the war contributed further to this.

At the end of the XIXth century, main roads (the RN 5, RN 6 and RN 7) were built crossing Burgundy from Paris to the south or the south-east following axes which still remain (the road to Switzerland through Dijon, the roads through the Yonne and Nièvre). The railway followed the Paris-Lyons-Mediterranean route via Dijon. The canals (the one from the river Marne to the river

Burgundy is also a land of welcome.

" I inherited a single wealth", wrote Edgard Varèse (1883-1965): "the memory of my grandfather in Burgundy". His first public work was called *Burgundy*. He spent his youth in Villars near Tournus (Saône-et-Loire). The artist Balthus lived in the château of Chassy at Montreuillon (Nièvre) from 1954 to the beginning of the '60s. He painted sixty works in this house, including his most important ones.

Saône was completed in 1907) were already under threat from road and rail transport. Agriculture was going through a difficult period and turning towards breeding and fattening Charolais cattle. The natural pastures were extended. After the phylloxera crisis, from the American aphid which destroyed the vines during the 1880's, ordinary table wines disappeared in favour of high quality vine-plants in a tiny production region.

The loss of steel from Lorraine had provoked a new industrial revolution in Burgundy (Commentry-Fourchambault, Montbard, the diversified Schneider empire which grew even more to an international scale).

Industrial Burgundy still meant the Pernot biscuit factory, Terrot bicycles and motorbikes, and also sugar works, wood industries, ceramics, textiles etc. But around 1930 there was a serious crisis, and many plants closed down. Chalon-sur-Saône became one of the most active industrial and trading centres. A bourgeois class based on economics built many factories there.

From the exodus of June 1940 to the Liberation combats of August and September 1944, the Second World War was felt deeply. The occupation was long and painful. Villages were flattened, martyred (Manlay and Comblanchien in the Côte-d'Or, Dun-les-Places in the Nièvre). The towns were heavily bombed (Châtillon-sur-Seine, Chenôve, Le Creusot, Nevers, Laroche-Migennes). At the end of the summer of 1944, Burgundy occupied a crucial strategic position for France. The allied forces which landed on June 6 in Normandy and August 15 in Provence joined up symbolically at Nod-sur-Seine (Châtillonais) on September 11, the 2nd Armoured Division meeting the 1st French Army. Thus the amalgam between the forces of the Resistance and the regular troops, to end the war.

"I belong to a country which I left", said Colette (1873-1954) born in Saint-Sauveur-en-Puisaye (Yonne) and who kept her Burgundy accent all her life including the richness of its words. Other authors from Burgundy at this time: Romain Rolland (1866-1944), born in Clamecy (Nièvre), Nobel prize for literature, author of the *Ame enchantée, Jean-Christophe, Colas Breugnon;* Marie Noël from Auxerre (1883-1968), one of the major poets of the XXth century. This epoch is also that of François Pompòn (1855-1933) born in Saulieu (Côte-d'Or) recognized as one of the masters of animal sculptures. And of Edouard Vuillard (1868-1940), born in Cuiseaux (Saône-et-Loire) and one of the greatest painters of his times.

The best steeplechasers in France are bred in Burgundy: here at Auteuil, Al Capone II, the richest steeplechasing horse in history (9.4 million French Francs prize-money). Photo D.R.

The following boom

Among other things, the baby-boom after the Liberation changed the demographic situation. Burgundy counted 1,440,000 inhabitants in 1962, and 1,500,000 in 1975. But was it going to reach the 1,694,000 inhabitants it had in 1987, when the population was at its peak? Growth brought it up to 160,000 inhabitants since 1945. It has benefitted from the development of the Dijon urban area and its student body. Saône-et-Loire (559,440 inhabitants), with its economic reconversion, has remained the most populated *département* of the region.

Around 1960 a unique phenomenon occurred. The rural population, which had not stopped falling since 1850 became fewer than the urban population, and the two curves are moving further and fur-

Saint-Bénigne Cathedral in Dijon and the new Fontaine d'Ouche urban area.

1,609,700 in 1990, but then there was stagnation. The Nièvre (233,300 inhabitants) continued to lose its population, a tendency which had continued for a whole century apart from a small increase in the years between 1950 and 1960. The Yonne (323,100 inhabitants) followed a different pattern. The north (Sénonais) saw an influx of population linked with the Ile-de-France, while the south lost its inhabitants. The Côte-d'Or (493,900 inhabitants) has gained ther apart. Immigration (about 90,000 persons of foreign origin) presents changing patterns. First of all there were Italians and Poles in the mines, and then there was a change of origin; from Portugal and Spain, Turkey, North Africa, Asia. At present those of foreign origin represent 5.5% of the total population, slightly lower than the national average, but they are divided unequally between the different towns and the different districts of the towns.

Right from the Liberation, the urban movement was accompanied by significant changes: the growth of industrial zones and housing developments (like les Grésilles and la Fontaine-d'Ouche in Dijon), university campuses, so-called dormitory areas on the edge of town etc. Village and local shops disappeared to be replaced by "department

Products from the land

Green Burgundy counted fewer than 30,000 exploitations in 1995 (62,500 in 1970), half of them in Saône-et-Loire. A quar-

Stag troating at dawn.
Photo D.R.

stores" (13 hypermarkets in 1982, 37 in 1995), bringing with them new forms of behaviour. The countryside often became isolated. One third of Burgundy has a population density of 10 persons per square kilometre (for the whole of Burgundy: 51, for France: 100). The population is ageing and there is less renewal for future generations.

ter are devoted to cattle breeding and meat, 20% to cereal farming, 15% to agriculture and stock-farming. Out of the 616,000 jobs in the region, 50,000 are linked with produce from the land (not counting mines and quarries). The constant fall in agricultural workers over the past half-century has been slightly less marked in Bur-

Roger Cuvillier, who invented the Pan-Cinor, the origin of the zoom-lens. Photo D.R.

where (394 million litres of milk, or 15% of French production in 1994). There are 1,300,000 heads of cattle mainly for meat production (lean animals produced by breeders who sell the cattle on the hoof to be fattened elsewhere, mainly in Italy). Cattle breeding in Burgundy has obtained brilliant results, particularly for export. The genetic quality of the reproductive animals is highly appreciated. Flocks of goats and sheep are on the decline. Bresse chickens are still known for their quality. The best horses (other than thoroughbreds) at the Auteil racecourse in Paris come from well-known Burgundian stables (Cercy-la-Tour in particular).

There are many other crops: sugar-beet in the valley of the Saône where vegetables (the onions of Auxonne) and horticulture (the chrysanthemums of Saint-Marcel) remain important. There are berries (blackcurrants, raspberries) in the Hautes-Côtes, orchards (the Marmotte cherry of the Auxerrois); gherkins from the Auxerrois etc. However, much of this produce is threatened by economic evolution and foreign competition.

Forest covers about 950,000 hectares (2,400,000 acres) of Burgundy, or 30% of its territory (5th among the regions of France). About 85% is hardwood forest. Burgundy oak (16% of the national production and the leading region of France) enjoys a high reputation. Conifers are progressing. A large part of production is sawn and processed in the region, but still not enough.

gundy (8% of jobs) than in the rest of France (6%). The modernisation and specialisation of these activities is often amazing. In the year 2000, there will be only 23,000 farms, for the rate at which they disappear does not change. Out of about 5 million acres used, arable land represents the half. These large farms of over 100 hectares (250 acres) produce cereals (mainly soft wheat, maize, barley), kolza especially in the Yonne and Côte-d'Or, sunflowers, peas (320,000 acres of set-aside out of the 2,175,000 used for all these crops in 1994). In the Nièvre the raising of milking cows has practically disappeared and is decreasing every-

Industrial decentralisation

Before becoming a political theme, decentralisation was already an economic reality. Near to Paris, well supplied with means of communication, plentiful and skilled manpower, Burgundy profited from a double boost from outside during the '50s and '60s. This was the arrival of capital from abroad (multinationals settling in Europe) and factories which did not have enough space in the Parisian belt.

Burgundy saw the arrival of several dozen enterprises (Kodak-Pathé at Chalon-sur-Saône; Thomson at Tonnerre and in the Saône Valley; Hoover, Sundstrand, New Holland, Winthrop etc. in Dijon) which created more than 25,000 new jobs. The policy of National Development then had a negative effect on this growth by orienting investments elsewhere. Recently, the world's industrial groups have been restructuring (departure of Hoover, with 800 jobs lost). The same is happening with French firms (the Seita factories in Dijon and Mâcon have closed). These problems come on top of the difficulties of the Schneider group (Creusot-Loire) in Saône-et-Loire which involve the disappearance of thousands of jobs.

But industrial Burgundy does not rely entirely on external support. Its advanced technology keeps up-to-date and active on a world scale: Imphy for iron-nickel-chrome alloys, Ugine Gueugnon for stainless steel, Iveco at

Chalon-sur-Saône, manufacture of the nucleus of atomic power stations.
Photo D.R.

Bourbon-Lancy for motors, Le Creusot for TGV bogies and nuclear engineering, Chalon-sur-Saône for nuclear engineering, like Montbard specializing in tubes, PSA in Dijon for the automobile industry etc. In 1953 the brothers Frédéric and Henri Lescure invented the pressure cooker which sold more than 50 million units and revolutionized women's lives and cooking. They turned a small ironmonger's in Selongey (Côte-d'Or) into the SEB group (Tefal, Calor, Rowenta). In Nevers the Look company became champion for ski fixations. In Chailley (Yonne), Gérard Bourgoin built up the second poultry

Chalon-sur-Saône, manufacture of T.G.V. bogies.
Photo D.R.

Painted wall in Dijon's covered market, by Dominique Maraval. Photo D.R.

Banga, Pampryl, Joker, Stypen etc. are part of Burgundy's heritage.

Industrial employment provides 26% of jobs, against 21% in the whole of France. Thus, the image of Burgundy as a non-industrial region is not correct. The mines closed at Le Creusot, then at Epinac (1966), La Machine (1974), and Blanzy-Montceau (in the '90s), the latter turning into an open-cast mine which fell from 900,000 tons in 1985 to only 500,000 tons in 1990. Only the Yom Kippur war boosted and prolonged this activity. The stone quarries (Châtillonnais and Tonnerois, Côte des vins) are still in activity because of the quality of the material, much appreciated by architects. The building industry is also well represented: 23,200 enterprises, with 45,000 employees.

Burgundy contributes 2.6% of the exports of France (14th Region out of the 22 of the metropolis). The top partners are Germany, then Italy and the United Kingdom.

firm in Europe (La Chaillotine) from a small family butcher's. Jean Le Lous and Bernard Majoie developed the pharmaceutical group of Fournier, in the Dijon urban area, to take the leading place in the world fight against cholesterol and introduced emergency surgical dressings (Urgo). Dim and Gerbe stockings, Clayeux children's clothes, and brand names as well known as

White collars

Public and private services make up 59% of jobs, against 65% in France in general. Even though their numbers have progressed rapidly, Burgundy has fewer service industries than the rest of France. Two thirds of the 40,000 jobs created during the '80s went to women. Between

1962 and 1990, the number of Burgundians with a job rose from 186,000 to 258,000, while 21,000 jobs for men disappeared. However, the rise in employment in the service industries could not compensate for the losses in agriculture and the building industry. Between 1965 and 1970 there was practically no unemployment in the region, but this appeared suddenly in the '80s, dropped between 1987 and 1990, to rise again, stabilize and fall back around 1994. In 1995 it involved some 80,000 persons, a level of about 9%.

In 1965, higher education involved 4,000 to 5,000 students. Thirty years later, the figure is over 40,000. The university campus of Dijon-Montmuzard, built at the beginning of the Vth Republic, the work of Rector Marcel Bouchard, was luckily designed for new extensions. After a slow-down in the building industry at the beginning of the '80s, the University 2000 Plan together with the financial aid of the Regional council made modernisation possible, whereas other sites (Le Creusot, Chalon-sur-Saône, Auxerre, Nevers) had new buildings. The Schools were extended: ENSAM (Arts and Metiers) at Cluny; ESC (Commerce and Administration of Enterprises) at Dijon; ENESAD (the third agronomy school of France) at Dijon. A National architectural school is planned for Dijon. In 1995 the CNRS created the European Institute of Taste Sciences in this city, to supplement the international axis of wine sciences and septentrional vineyards. Nevers has a higher school specialized in the automobile and transport.

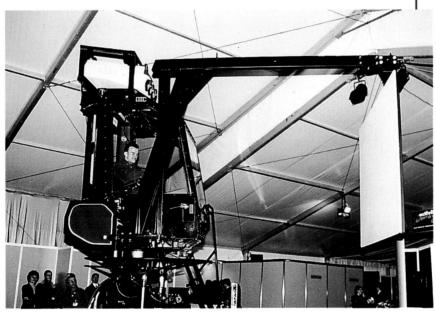

Simulation tree-feller made by the Higher National Polytechnic of "Arts et Metiers" of Cluny. Photo D.R.

Seven-league boots

Burgundy is developing its position as a crossroads of communication, an indispensable advantage for its economic development (Europe's terrestrial port). Enterprises are working more and more on the hand-to-mouth principle. They have to receive and deliver in less than a day for the whole of neighbouring Europe.

the Paris-Lyons A 6 (1970) motorway one can count 200 kilometres between 1975 and 1995, the A 36 Mulhouse-Beaune (1980), the A 31 Dijon-Beaune, the A 31 Nancy-Dijon (1981), the A 5 Troyes-Langres-Dijon, Dijon-Dole (1995) the A 40 Mâcon-Geneva, the A 39 Dole-Bourg-en-Bresse (1998), Dordives-Cosne-sur-Loire (1999). The seven-league boots have found their place on the lands of Burgundy, the first region to accept the Paris-South-East TGV (High-Speed

The busiest motorway and railway in France.

Although the fluvial link from the North Sea to the Mediterranean is now from Fos-sur-Mer to Auxonne (Côte-d'Or) for convoys up to 5,000 tons (Freycinet barges are from 180 to 200 tons), the junction with Alsace has still to be completed. The project was brought up again in 1994. With over 550 kilometres of motorway, Burgundy is one of the best-served regions of France and even of Europe. After

Train) in 1981 and already preparing for the Dijon-Mulhouse (Rhine-Rhône) TGV in the year 2010. The sorting office of Perrigny-Gevrey-Chambertin is the second largest of the country. And as for the old Jean-Behra racing circuit of Magny-Cours (Nièvre) it has become a huge Formula One complex and hosts the French Grand Prix which was formerly on the Dijon-Prenois circuit.

Filmed in Burgundy

∽ *Les Amants*, Louis Malle (1958) in Dijon and the Ouche valley (Côte-d'Or).

∽ *Angélique, marquise des Anges*, Bernard Borderie (1964) at Fontenay and Marigny-le-Cahouët (Côte-d'Or).

∽ *La Belle Américaine*, Robert Dhéry (1961) at Sens (Yonne).

∽ *Calmos*, Bertrand Blier (1976) in the Ouche valley (Côte-d'Or).

∽ *Le Capitan*, André Hunebelle (1960) in Avallon (Yonne).

∽ *Le Cercle Rouge*, Jean-Pierre Melville (1970) in Saint-Loup-de-Varennes (Saône-et-Loire).

∽ *Clérambard*, Yves Robert (1969) at Semur-en-Auxois and Marigny-le-Cahouët (Côte-d'Or).

∽ *Conte d'hiver*, Eric Rohmer (1992) at Nevers (Nièvre).

∽ *Coup de tête*, Jean-Jacques Annaud (1979) at Auxerre (Yonne).

∽ *Cyrano de Bergerac*, Jean-Paul Rappenau (1990) at Dijon and Fontenay (Côte-d'Or).

∽ *Father Brown*, Robert Hamer (1954) at Cluny and in the Mâconnais.

∽ *L'Empreinte des géants*, Robert Enrico (1980) on the A 36 motorway works near Seurre.

∽ *Une Femme fidèle*, Roger Vadim (1976) at Tracy-sur-Loire (Nièvre).

∽ *La Grande Vadrouille*, Gérard Oury (1966) in the Yonne, the Nièvre and the Côte-d'Or (Meursault, Beaune).

∽ *Hiroshima mon Amour*, Alain Resnais (1959), Nevers (Nièvre).

∽ *Jeanne la Pucelle - Les Batailles*, Jacques Rivette (1994) in the Côte-d'Or (Grosbois-en-Montagne which became... Orléans etc.) and in Saône-et-Loire (Verdun-sur-le-Doubs).

∽ *Mon Oncle Benjamin*, Edouard Molinaro (1969), Vézelay, Avallon etc. (Yonne and Nièvre).

∽ *Ni vu ni connu*, Yves Robert (1958), Semur-en-Auxois (Côte-d'Or - the first big role of Louis de Funès).

∽ *Partir, Revenir...*, Claude Lelouch (1985), Châteauneuf-en-Auxois (Côte-d'Or).

∽ *La Passion de Bernadette*, Jean Delannoy (1989), Nevers (Nièvre).

∽ *Poil de carotte*, Julien Duvivier (1932), Lormes, Chirtry-les-Mines, etc. (Nièvre).

∽ *La Reine Margot*, Patrice Chéreau (1994), Maulnes and Cruzy-le-Châtel (Yonne).

∽ *Le Repos du Guerrier*, Roger Vadim (1962), Dijon.

∽ *Happy Road*, Gene Kelly (1960), Semur-en-Auxois (Côte-d'Or).

∽ *Le Souffle au coeur*, Louis Malle (1971), Saint-Honoré-les-Bains (Nièvre).

∽ *Tatie Danielle*, Etienne Chatiliez (1990), Auxerre (Yonne).

∽ *Les Trois Mousquetaires*, Bernard Borderie (1961), Montbard and the Auxois (Côte-d'Or).

∽ *Les Valseuses*, Bertrand Blier (1974), the Ouche valley (Côte-d'Or).

∽ *La Veuve Couderc*, Pierre Granier-Deferre (1971), Cheuge (Côte-d'Or).

Filming *Cyrano de Bergerac* with Gerard Depardieu and Anne Brochet, La Chouette street in Dijon. Photo D.R.

Verrerie street in Dijon: still medieval.

DIJON GREW BUT SAVED ITS SOUL

Burgundy's capital knew how to expand, develop and modernize,
without losing its soul. Research and high-tech industries,
side-by-side with a city of art and history which is part of Europe's heritage.

I s there any other town or city where one can make a rendezvous by saying "We'll meet on the corner of the Mirror..."? The Corner of the Mirror, the main crossroads of the Old Town, owes its name to a house which is now no longer there. But a few steps away, the House with Three Faces saw Charles the Bold pass by when he made his entry into Dijon five centuries ago.

The Corner of the Mirror describes the feeling of Dijon very well, attached as it is to its rich past as a city of art and history and a heritage preserved with passion. It has resumed its vocation as capital of Burgundy, situated at the crossing-point of yesterday and tomorrow, with its cultural exchanges and economic relations. The Burgundian plateau suddenly falls away to the plain of the river Saône. Dijon is a certainly a town to stop for a while, a halt, a resting place. The town has understood how to expand without losing its soul.

Lucky rendezvous

Several times in its history, Dijon has been lucky. Since it was open to the whole of European culture, the Dukes of Burgundy chose it as capital. It reaped all the advantages with none of the disadvantages. It was far away from the military conflicts and could devote itself to the arts. When it became French, it kept its freedoms, spread its influence across the province and took an active part in the joys of the spirit (Rameau, Bossuet, Saint Jeanne de Chantal, Buffon, the president de Brosses and Jean-Jacques Rousseau are not exactly a poor pantheon).

Panoramic view
of Burgundy's capital city.

The Revolution shook this moderate town, which nonetheless saw the passage of Carnot, Prieur de la Côte-d'Or, Monge, Guyton de Morveau (founders of the Ecole Polytechnique). At that time Dijon had to be content as the *département's* chief town. Officially, Burgundy no longer existed... nonetheless Dijon never gave up. Its population quadrupled in a century and doubled again the following century to reach the 150,000 inhabitants it has today, 250,000 if one counts the whole of the urban area.

Would the Paris-Lyons railway run through Dijon? Yes, after a fierce struggle, and this made the town's modern fortune. Just after the war of 1870, Alsace and Lorraine changed flag. Dijon became a town which was almost a border town, fortified, full of soldiers and repatriates from the East, giving it an economic boost.

Formerly Dijon had been appreciated for its spirit (Piron, La Monnoye). In the XXth century other charms were discovered. Gaston Gérard, the mayor between the two wars, reshaped the image of the city by creating the Gastronomic Fair on the model of the Fair conceived by Edouard Herriot at Lyons when it was quite new. He multiplied his travels to "sell" his city. He kept open house. With Curnonsky at their head, the whole press visited Dijon to enjoy the good cheer. To put it briefly, he happily stuck a fork into the back of the city, which had become a town for good eating and good drinking. The whole Côte rivalled each other in ardour (Tastevin, wine auctions in the Hospices de

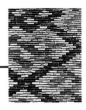

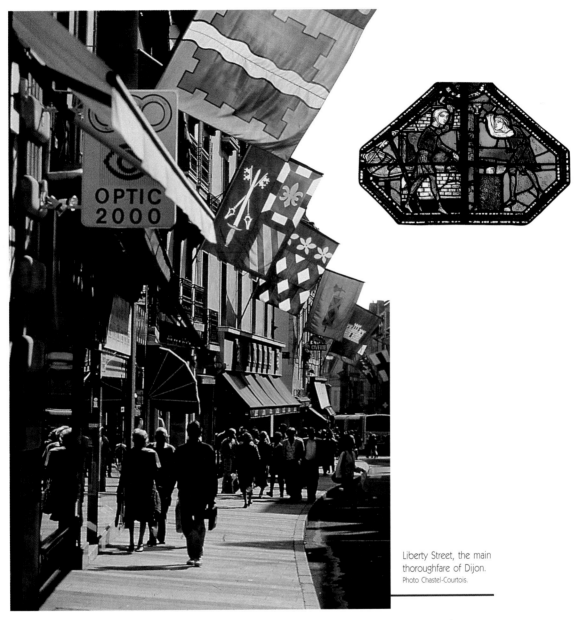

Liberty Street, the main
thoroughfare of Dijon.
Photo Chastel-Courtois.

Beaune, Paulée de Meursault, etc.).

Then, after the Second World War, Canon Félix Kir arrived. He was elected deputy mayor of Dijon at the age of 69! And he was to stay there for twenty-three years. He was a legendary figure, and not just because he gave his name to an aperitif. His vision was wide and grandiose. Dijon only had 3,000 students at that time and yet, with the rector Marcel Bouchard, he created a modern campus for 30,000 students, even including huge parking lots although the lecturers themselves were still using their bicycles (Montmuzard). He had imagination, and imposed one of his fixed

Churches

- Saint-Bénigne Cathedral: the abbey church of a monastery founded in the VIth century at the time of the cult of Saint Bénigne who evangelised Dijon. There were two successive basilicas, and then the Romanesque edifice built by Guillaume de Volpiano just after the year 1000 (the crypt still exists). Finally, the present church (end of the XIIIth, beginning of the XIVth century). The spire (end of the XIXth); a freestanding pyramid of 55 metres (183 ft) is the highest in France.
- Saint-Philibert: old church being restored. Romanesque parts (main porch) and XVth century. Stone bell tower from the XVIth century.
- Notre-Dame: built at the beginning of the XIIIth century, restored in the XIXth. Its originality lies in its three ranges of gargoyles on the façade which amazed Henry Miller in his *Tropic of Cancer.* Le Jacquemart (clock with figurines) comes from Courtrai (1382) where it was on the belfry. The Black Virgin (polychrome in reality) from the XIth century, the protector of Dijon (Notre-Dame du Bon Espoir) which inspired André Malraux.
- Saint-Michel: an amazing Renaissance façade on a Flamboyant Gothic edifice (XVth and XVIth centuries).
- Saint-Etienne: the present Chamber of Commerce and Industry, the former cathedral before Saint-Bénigne, dating from the XIth century and altered many times (its tympanum is now in Saint-Bénigne).
- Saint-Jean: the church where Bossuet was baptised, which has been turned into a theatre (The Burgundy National Theatre), dating from the middle of the XVth century. Chapels: Godrans, Sainte-Anne, Carmélites.

The Black Virgin of Notre-Dame (XIth century): "an unprecedented work of art" as André Malraux wrote.

ideas: a lake. At the municipal council, he was the only one to vote in favour. He declared "Motion adopted!". And these days it is the most beautiful way of arriving in Dijon.

At the beginning of the seventies, Dijon made the jump and launched several new projects under Robert Poujade. The renovations produced one of the finest historic centres of France, spared by the wars, and offering the visitor a review of a thousand years of architecture, like an open book. It is one of the greenest cities in France, with dozens of parks and gardens quite apart from the Arque-

Notre-Dame of Dijon.

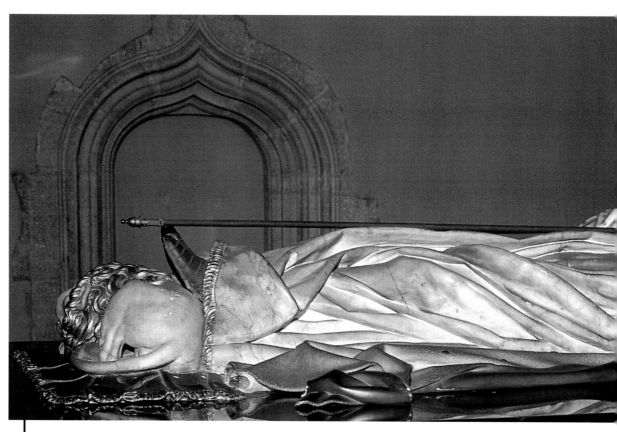

The tombs
of Philip
the Bold
and John
the Fearless
in Dijon's Fine
Arts Museum.

Right:
Palace of the
Dukes and the
States of Burgundy.

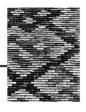

Civil architecture

The Palace of the Dukes and the States of Burgundy: this palace was built on the extensive remains still existing from the palace of the Dukes of the House of Valois (Bar tower, 1365; ducal kitchens, 1433; Philip the Good tower, 1443). It was built between the end of the XVIIth century and the Revolution, facing the Place Royale where the equestrian statue of Louis XIV then stood, by Jules-Hardouin-Mansart and the architects of Versailles and Paris (staircase built by Jacques Gabriel in 1735, chapel of the Elected Members, States and Flore halls, etc.). Mansions and homes from the Middle Ages: Hôtel Chambellan, rue des Forges and Hôtel Thomas Berbisey, rue Berbisey (Flamboyant Gothic style); the House with Three Faces, rue de la Liberté; the Millière house, rue de la Chouette (owl); Verrerie and Chaudronnerie streets. Renaissance mansions and homes: the Maillard house, rue des Forges; the Caryatids house, Chaudronnerie street; Hôtel Le Compasseur, rue Vannerie.
Mansions of the Classical Epoch: Hôtel de Vogüé, rue de la Chouette; Hôtel Bouhier de Savigny and the Hôtel Legouz de Gerland, rue Vauban; Hôtel Chartraire de Montigny and the Hôtel of the military commander, rue Vannerie; Hôtel Bouhier de Lantenay, rue de la Préfecture (the present Prefect's Residence); Hôtel Févret de Saint-Mesmin, Place Bossuet; Hôtel des Barres, rue Chabot-Charny; Hôtel Fyot de Mimeure, rue Amiral-Roussin.
Protected sector: 100 hectares (250 acres) and about fifty mansions belonging to the Parliament and the States of Burgundy in the XVIIth and XVIIIth centuries.
XIXth century: the theatre (Restoration period), the Markets, Darcy Square, Saint-Bernard Square (second half of the XIXth century).

The Vogüé mansion.

Museum

⚬ Fine-Arts Museums ⚬
The heritage of the Dukes of Burgundy (tombs with mourners of Philip the Bold and John the Fearless, altar pieces by Jacques de Baerze, Flemish primitives and *Nativity* by the Master of Flémalle), impressive collections and the Granville donation (from Georges de La Tour to Nicolas de Staël).
Big exhibitions in the summer.
Musée Magnin: the atmosphere of the mansions of the art-lovers of the beginning of the XXth century.
He himself was advisor to the Audit Office while she was painter and critic. Brother and sister.

⚬ Archeological museum ⚬
In the former Benedictine Abbey of Saint-Bénigne, several remarkable items (the Blanot treasure, the La Rochepot treasure, statues from the springs of the Seine, etc.).

⚬ Museum of sacred art ⚬
In a former church built around 1700 by the Bernadines, the treasure of the sacred art of the Côte-d'Or.

⚬ Museum of Burgundy Life ⚬
Perrin-de-Puycousin:
within the buildings and cloisters of this former monastery (Museum of sacred art - Sainte-Anne), the Dijon of former times and Burgundian rural life, following a chronological circuit.

⚬ Natural History Museum ⚬
The museum is very modern and attractive in design and possesses several unique items (like the fossil glyptodon from the Argentinian pampas).

⚬ Open-air Museum ⚬
The Montmuzard university campus is adorned with sculptures by Arman, Agam, Karel Appel, Gottfried Honegger, etc.,
Contemporary Art: the FRAC (Regional Fund) and the Consortium.

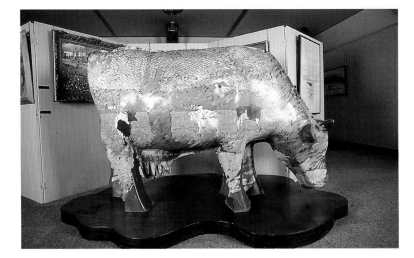

From top to bottom, left to right:
Jack-o'-the-clock, altarpiece by Jacques de Baërze, work by Karel Appel in the university campus, one of the paintings from the *Footballers* series by Nicolas de Staël (photo D.R.), Buri's cow landscape (photo Chastel-Courtois).

buse Botanical Gardens and Colombière Park.

The city knew how to profit from the exceptional motorway and railway knot to develop itself as the land port of Europe with the Saône Valley. At the century's end, it will add a Palace of Congresses and an auditorium, thus completing an economic vocation specialized in pharmaceuticals, the automobile, food-processing, etc.

A rendezvous with luck? "Have you touched the owl?" they say in Dijon the day before an exam or a wedding. This is the little stone owl on one of the flying buttresses of Notre-Dame. Is it the signature of the architect or the mark of a Companion? No-one knows. House-wives returning from market, lovers hand in hand and even the gendarme making his rounds, everyone "touches the owl" affectionately, stroking the bird of wisdom and making a wish. Several of the scenes from the film *Cyrano* were shot in this road of the Owl.

These days, Dijon is once again the capital of Burgundy. Kingdom, duchy, province, it has now become a Region.

The owl of Notre-Dame: stroking it brings luck. Photo D.R.

Gardens and Parks

ᴄᴏ Colombière Park ᴄᴏ
This extends over 34 hectares (85 acres), and was created around 1680 by the Condé family (governors of Burgundy up until the Revolution). The work of Antoine de Maerle, pupil of Le Nôtre, it is a fine example of a French-style park. *Travels in France* of Henry James ends on a bench in this park.

ᴄᴏ Arquebuse ᴄᴏ
One of the richest botanical gardens in the world, with its 3,500 varieties divided into 66 sections, created in 1871 and transferred here in 1833. Arboretum.

ᴄᴏ Darcy Garden ᴄᴏ
Urbanism of the XIXth century, in the Napoleon III style, in harmony with the square. *The Bear*, by the Burgundian sculptor François Pompon, is the replica of the work which made him famous at the Autumn Salon of 1922.

ᴄᴏ Dukes' Square ᴄᴏ
The former garden of Margaret of Flanders, wife of Philip the Bold, next to his former palace.

ᴄᴏ Lake Kir ᴄᴏ
A work of patience. Canon Félix Kir dreamed about it when he was a young seminarist in 1895. In 1945, at the age of 69, the sash of mayor of Dijon allowed him to put his dream into practice. He devoted nineteen years of effort to complete it in 1964. The monumental statue of *The Grenadier*, the work of Georges Diébelt, used to stand under the Alma Bridge in Paris, next to the statue of the Zouave who now plays the role of rain-gauge for the capital.

ᴄᴏ Combe à la Serpent Park ᴄᴏ
326 hectares (815 acres) of nature park and quarries (1976) due to the talent of Andre Holodynski.

ᴄᴏ Canal Port ᴄᴏ
Created at the end of the XVIIIth century on the Burgundy canal, it still harbours pleasure boats in beautiful surroundings dominated by the obelisk (1786) placed to commemorate the link between the seas through this canal. Gustave Eiffel was born in 1832 near the port.

THE WINE OF BURGUNDY, OR THE LONGEST REIGN IN HISTORY

No wine in the world has ever reigned so long, nearly two thousand years of glory, from harvest to harvest, vintage to vintage. A few drops of good wine in the sea from the vineyards. But what a figurehead bottle!

For every 250 bottles of wine produced in the world only one is from Burgundy. But this bottle is the figurehead on the prow, in the ocean of products made from the vine! "The longest reign in history", according to Raymond Dumay. Without doubt, the vine was introduced here several centuries before Christ by Gauls from Italy and was already ancient in the IVth century A.D. (the first known description here). No other vineyards have retained their glory for two thousand years.

Success is due to the perfect harmony between the earth and the vine-plant, associated with the talent of men. Although they cover a mere 50,000 acres, the Burgundy vineyards spread across three *départements:* the Yonne (Chablisian, Auxerrois, the vineyards of Joigny, Vézelay et Tonnerre); the Côte-d'Or (Côte de Nuits, Côte de Beaune, Hautes-Côtes); the Saône-et-Loire (Côte Chalonnaise, Maranges, Couchois, Mâconnais). Beaujolais, united with Burgundy in principle, has acquired its own autonomy although part of these vineyards are situated in Saône-et-Loire (Moulin-à-Vent, Saint-Amour, Fleurie). As for the Nièvre vineyards (Pouilly-Fumé in particular), these are logically associated with the Val de Loire wine-growing industry. In all, this makes up 165 million bottles a year. One out of two is exported.

Exceptional soil

Based on limestone mixed with clay and marl, but with countless nuances, the vineyards are usually situated on the slopes facing the rising sun or south-east, at an altitude of between 200 and 300 metres (670-1,000 ft). They are divided into thousands of *climats*, or "climates". This Burgundian notion defines a plot of land with its own specific properties (soil, subsoil, exposure, etc.) and identified by the same name for centuries. Le Clos de Bèze at Gevrey-Chambertin thus became part of history in the year 640. Le Clos de Vougeot was born at the very beginning of the XIIth century.

The earth has always taken precedence over ownership. When guaranteed vintages were introduced in the '30s, other wine-growing areas chose the property, the trade name or the vine-plant as reference. But Burgundy, quite correctly, chose the land. It can seem like a complete maze, with so many different *climats*. But the personality of the wine depends on them, as does its quality.

Photo D.R.

Harvest festival
in the Mâconnais,
by Carteron called
Charles (1856).
Photo Jean-Pierre Coqueau.

The excellence of the plants

Burgundy does not produce blended wines, from mixing several varieties of grape together. It has always produced unadulterated batches. As the cradle of two varieties which have become universal, it devotes itself above all to the Chardonnay for white and Pinot Noir for red. In Mâconnais one can add the Gamay Noir with white juice, which already heralds Beaujolais, and also a dry white wine, Aligoté.

Romanée Conti, Chambertin, Clos-Vougeot, Corton... Pinot Noir, which covers 8000 hectares (20,000 acres) here, is the finest and most fragile of the varieties for red wine (its juice is colourless and during vinification it is the skin which gives it its colour). It produces sumptuous wines, full-bodied and rich, complex and subtle. There are variations of the "Black", such as Beurot, Liébault, and like all other varieties of vine-plants, there are endless clones whose selection is continually being improved.

Montrachet, Chablis, Meursault, Pouilly-Fuissé... With 9000 hectares (22,500 acres) in Burgundy, the Chardonnay plant (called the Beaunois in Chablis) offers a unity of white grapes to the vineyards yet without any uniformity. In effect, a thousand variations on the same theme. Mellow and dry, firm and caressing, it expresses all the graces within an inflexible character. Vigorous and

Château de Gevrey-Chambertin: the "fortified cellar" of Cluny's monks in Côte de Nuits.

Above: Grape harvest near Dijon in the XVIIIth century.
Painting by Jean-Baptiste Lallemand.
Photo D.R.

A pyramid of guarantees

Burgundy depends more than anywhere else on the idea of guaranteed origin, with a quarter of the AOC of France (appellation d'origine contrôlée), or 110 out of 400. Such a diversity is not really surprising: each Burgundy wine carries its own particular name.

The *grands crus*, or best vintages, count 1% of production. There are 32 in the Côte-d'Or plus one in Chablis (which has seven different *climats* or sections). At the summit of the Burgundy pyramid are: Chablis grand cru Grenouille - Clos de Bèze, Chambertin, Corton-Charlemagne, Bâtard-Montrachet.

The first or *premiers crus*, comprising 11% of production, are AOCs from local communes when their *climat* is classed as *premier cru* (561 *climats* in this situation). Examples: Chablis - Mont de Milieu, Nuits-Saint-Georges - Les-Saint-Georges, Beaune - Grèves, Mercurey - Clos du Roi.

The other AOCs from the communes (53 in total) represent 23% of production and constitute the "Villages" vintages. The name of the *climat* may figure on the label. Examples: Chablis, Gevrey-Chambertin, Pommard, Rully, Pouilly-Fuissé. Petit-Chablis is a commune AOC.

Finally, 65% of Burgundy production is at the base of the pyramid; the regional AOCs: 22 at the moment. Examples: Bourgogne, Mâcon, etc.

There are thus three category levels: the *grands crus*; the communal vintages (*Villages* and *premiers crus*) followed or not by the name of the *climat*; and the regional vintages (often incorrectly called "generic"). These refer either to the variety of vine (Bourgogne Aligoté, Bourgogne Passetoutgrain - from at least one third Pinot grapes - and Gamay), or to a method of preparation (Crémant de Bourgogne produced by the Champagne method), or to a geographic origin (Bourgogne Chitry, Bourgogne Hautes-Côtes de Nuits et de Beaune, Bourgogne Côte Chalonnaise). For red, white and rosé, the origin is called Burgundy, without any other indication apart sometimes from the authorized name of the *climat* (Montre-Cul for example at Dijon-Chenôve).

Arcenant in the Hautes Côtes de Nuits, Vergy country.

Nuits-Saint-Georges, the heart of the Côte-d'Or.
Wine-grower inspecting his cellar (XIXth century painting). Photo Chesnay

generous, this variety is afraid of one thing only; spring frosts.

Gamay Noir with its white juice gives a delicate red wine, light yet fruity. It is a robust and productive variety, with a marked preference for the acid soils found in the south of Burgundy (6,200 acres for the ensemble of the vineyards) and also in the Beaujolais region. There has always been trench warfare between Gamay Noir and Pinot

Noir. Gamay offers a more abundant wine, easier to produce, more profitable for the wine-grower, while the abbeys, the upper class producers, preferred Pinot Noir, perhaps better but less prolific and providing a less reliable income. Since the Middle Ages the Pinot and the Gamay have represented a social conflict as much as an oenological rivalry. These days this has all calmed down.

Aligoté is to Chardonnay what Gamay is to Pinot. A white wine which is more straightforward, full of life, sharp as flint and fresh as a spring breeze. It obligingly extends over about 3,200 acres, and in Bouzeron (Côte Chalonnaise) it has even managed to earn its own guarantee of origin. The Hautes-Côtes suit it well.

In the Yonne there are still some very old varieties. For white, the Melon of Burgundy (Nantais Muscadet); the Sauvignon of Saint-Bris; le Sacy. For red, the César whose last ranks hold out at Irancy.

Clos de Vougeot château.
Photo C. Sarramon.

Brotherhood of the Tastevin Knights

These days there are countless wine and gastronomy brotherhoods.
Founded in 1934, the Brotherhood of the Tastevin Knights is the oldest of all.
This is an idea from Burgundy itself.
At the time, wine was not selling well. Several inhabitants of Nuits-Saint-Georges
decided to react: "Since no-one wants our wines,
we'll invite our friends and drink them together!".
Since they had to find a pretext, they invented a brotherhood,
a Burgundian baptism. Success was not long to follow. The brothers, with the triple
badge on their shoulder ("Noah, father of wine; Bacchus, god of wine;
Saint Vincent, patron of wine-growers") soon became
the best propagandists of wines from Burgundy.
This was when public relations were first invented!
The Brotherhood of the Tastevin Knights holds its Chapters (twenty per year)
in the Clos de Vougeot château acquired in 1994. It has 10,000 members and many
Commanders in the four quarters of the globe. It has often shown the way.
Thus the Tastevinage or tasting which, after an anonymous and strict tasting picks out
the wines "which one would like to offer one's friends"
(these wines are called tastevinés)
or again the "Turning Saint-Vincent".
Since the XIXth century, most of the wine-growers' villages have had a mutual-assistance
society, generally created - even though often laic - under the patronage of
Saint Vincent. Thus, any wine-grower who is unable to "do his vines" either through accident or
illness, is helped by his colleagues. The statue of the patron saint is housed by a different family
each year: it "turns". In 1937, the Brotherhood of the Tastevin Knights organized an annual
assembly of all the Burgundian brotherhoods of Saint Vincent, on the last Saturday of January,
in a different village each time and prepared several years ahead: the Turning Saint-Vincent,
the best and warmest of all the wine-growers' celebrations.
Burgundy has seen the arrival and the development of many other brotherhoods:
Piliers Chablisiens, Trois Ceps, Foudres du Tonnerrois, Veilleurs de Nuits,
Cousinerie de Bourgogne at Savigny-lès-Beaune, Bailliage de Pommard,
Grumeurs de Santenay, Disciples de la Chanteflûte at Mercurey,
Compagnons de Saint Vincent in the Mâconnais, etc.

Tastevin en main

Confrérie des Chevaliers du Tastevin

Photo D.R.

The songsters of the Brotherhood of the Tastevin Knights,
the Cadets of Burgundy. Photo D.R.

The personality of the vintage

Each vintage has its own special features. More or less successful, more or less generous. These differences can be ex-

After the snows, the risk of spring frosts: braziers to protect the vines.

plained by a multitude of factors, particularly climatic, which change and evolve for each vintage. Apart from a few exceptions, wines from Burgundy are not young wines, to be drunk only a few months after the

harvest. They must be matured. The bottling comes one to two years later. Usually a wine from Burgundy is considered ready after 3 to 4 years. This is a wine to be laid down and which can be superb after ten to fifteen years, wonderful after fifty (for example, those from 1947 and '49 which we are drinking now).

There is also the fact that wine is the work of man. The influence of the wine-maker - the

106

wine grower often assisted by an oenologist - is a determining factor. Either the wine-grower sells him by a dealer who then matures and markets it; or the wine is produced by a coopera-

Pinot Noir,
the vine-plant of one
of the great red wines
of Burgundy.

his wine directly, and it is then called after the name of his property; or his wine is bought from tive (like Chablis, or Hautes-Côtes, and many from Saône-et-Loire).

Mâconnais landscape.

Right: Photo D.R.

Down to the cellars

One of Burgundy's special rites is the descent to the cellar. A tasting accompanied by personal commentaries. This ceremony is carried out in a special place, where the wines of the owner or wine-merchant are matured. There is no singing here. Tasting is serious. One savours the wine in a glass or, even better, in one's own *tâtevin* (or wine-taster). Often one passes from barrel to barrel for young wines, and takes several bottles of the most mature wines. Then one can compare the *crus*, the vintages, while learning the art of tasting.

Burgundy has a precise and evocative vocabulary for the endless nuances of the colour (limpid, colour, reflections etc.), of the nose (the universe of vegetal, floral, fruity, mineral aromas, etc.) and of the mouth (body, consistency, aftertaste, etc). The ideal is called complexity.

Auctions at the Hospices de Beaune and Nuits-Saint-Georges are "candle-lit". The lot goes to the highest bidder when the last candle burns out.

Photo D.R.

Wine auction at the Hospices de Beaune

The Hôtel-Dieu de Beaune, founded in 1443 by Nicolas Rolin, possesses a big wine-growing domain (more than 60 hectares, or 150 acres) the result of donations. It is divided between Côte de Beaune, Côte de Nuits and Pouilly-Fuissé vineyards. Since 1859, the Hospices wines have been auctioned on the third Sunday of each November following the harvest. "The greatest charity auction in the world" has become a major event, giving an indication about the market but also demanding much higher prices. It is one of the three days of the Trois Glorieuses: the evening before, a Chapter of the Knights of the Tastevin Brotherhood; the next day, the Paulée de Meursault (end of harvest lunch) and its literary prize. The Hospices of Nuits-Saint-Georges also auction their wines in the Spring following the harvest.

Former mansion of the Dukes of Burgundy, a wine museum these days.

Dijon Municipal
Library. Cistercian
manuscript,
early
XIIth century.

Visits

All the Burgundy vineyards are on the Wine Roads, offering a welcome and tasting in each village. The Interprofessional Office of the wines of Burgundy publishes a guide of wines and cellars, giving the addresses of dealers, and wine-growing cooperatives which accept visitors (many cellars).

Other visits:

Bailly (hamlet of Saint-Bris-le-Vineux, Yonne)
Former stone quarries converted into *caveau*, or cellar where the Crémant de Bourgogne is prepared.

At Saint-Bris-le-Vineux
House of the Auxerrois Vine.

Beaune (Côte-d'Or)
Burgundy wine museum and former Mansion of the Dukes of Burgundy; the whole city is dedicated to the cult of wine.

Chalon-sur-Saône (Saône-et-Loire)
Wine Centre of the Côte chalonnaise.

Chenôve (Côte-d'Or)
XVth century presses in the King's House.

Clos-Vougeot (Côte-d'Or)
Former château of the abbot of Cîteaux, where the Brotherhood of the Tastevin Knights organizes its Chapters and Tastings, and which still has the old cellar dating back to the XIIIth century, and the fermenting room built in the XIVth and XVth centuries like a cloister, with enormous presses.

Cuiseaux (Saône-et-Loire)
Vine and Wine Centre, built in memory of a vineyard which no longer exists.

Mâcon (Saône-et-Loire)
Centre of Mâconnais wines.

Marey-leè-Fussey (Côte-d'Or)
Hautes-Côtes Centre.

Pouilly-sur-Loire (Nièvre)
Loire vineyards in Burgundy (Château de Nozet).

Romanèche-Thorins (Saône-et-Loire)
Wine Hamlet created by Georges Duboeuf.

Photo Didier Benaouda.

AT THE HEART OF TASTE: THE GASTRONOMIST'S PARADISE

It is easy to understand why the culinary palette offered by Burgundy is pleasing to the palate. Art and pleasure combine to provide taste, local delicacies, colours, scents and savours.

More than two centuries ago, the writer and gastronomist Brillat-Savarin praised the Burgundians for their "silken stomachs", since he was so impressed by the virtues of their cooking. Among the fine-arts, those of the table have always been rated very highly here. Where do receptions take place these days in the Dijon Town Hall? In the Ducal kitchens, a model of architecture, designed for preparing the fabulous banquets offered by the Grand Dukes of Burgundy. Recipes are handed down from mother to daughter and are precious family secrets.

Photo A. Doire.

Colours, odours, flavours

Burgundy has a special feel about it, just as France has. This is made up of different colours, different odours, different flavours, a thousand and one pleasures which are often comestible, a culture in itself. Conversation is considered as a culinary art. One savours with contemplation; sometimes murmuring a compliment, or making a remark. As for the visitor, he should avoid arriving at a quarter to twelve if he is not expected. The cook herself has to be left in peace, to have the time to go to market, and your host must be able to go down to the cellar and pick out the bottles he has chosen for you and which will be opened in your honour. To put it briefly, the time required to live well... takes time.

Burgundy has a heritage which is irreplaceable. Its earth, its climate, the countryside, traditions, local and loyal customs, guarantees of origin, the people still have faith in the spirit of their culture. Wine is not the only product from here; there are also cereals and vegetables, meat from the Charolais cattle and the chickens from Bresse, red berries (cherries, gooseberries, raspberries, strawberries) and black berries (blackcurrant, blackberry), and cheeses. Often this produce, with its special taste, carries the name of its place of origin: the Appoigny gherkin, the Auxonne onion, the Auxerrois cherry, or the Hautes-Côtes blackcurrant.

Local know-how accentuates the excellence of the products. This is the very heart of Burgundy which, for example, took centuries to breed the splendid race of white Charolais cattle - whose cradle is in Brionnais - Charolais and in

Opposite page:
Yonne cherry and Aligoté tart,
Charlotte of red berries and spiced bread.
Photo Didier Benaouda.

The Charolais breed

The development of the race of Charolais cattle is the result of a special and innovative tradition of breeding. The XVIIIth century farmers of the Brionnais were very advanced in the science of fattening horned cattle in their meadows. The animals were bought lean at the end of the winter and put out into the pastures as soon as spring came, to gain weight. The quality of the earth, the abundance of grass and the climatic conditions of this part of Southern Burgundy contribute to this specialisation, unique in the history of rural France. The origins of the present strength and power of the Charolais beef cattle begin here. The rapid economic development of rural France in the XVIIIth century was accompanied by new habits: meat consumption went up in the towns, Paris and Lyons in particular, even though it remained a luxury product only for the rich bourgeoisie and the nobility. Around 1750, in the Brionnais, the first agricultural company was created when two of the biggest merchant-fattening families of the region became associates; the Despierres and the Montmessin. They could be present at seven fairs in the same day, between the Morvan and the Auvergne, thanks to their powerful network of middlemen. The accounts were made every year on Saint-Martin's day, November 11th. The marketing was carried out on the hoof. The herds were driven using the methods of American cowboys. This required a great deal of organization for relays, so that the daily journeys were relatively short to avoid the animals losing too much weight. They took twelve days to reach Paris, leaving from the rallying point of Cosne-sur-Loire, a distance of 500 km (312 miles). The Charolais cow, a descendant of the south-east branch of the Jurassic race of central Europe, is white or cream in colour, with nostrils which are pale and unspotted. She has a wide forehead, round and light-coloured horns, big cheeks, a wide muzzle, a stocky neck, a deep chest, a horizontal muscled back, very wide loins, with legs squarely placed and a skin which is medium thick and supple. The height to the withers varies from between 1.35 metres (4.5 ft) and 1.45 metres (4.8 ft) and the weight varies from 700 to 1,200 kg (1,540-2,640 lbs) for cows as against 1,000 to 1,650 kg (2,200-3,630 lbs) for males. The Charolais race is very important to the economy of Burgundy. Charolais cows represent 25% of the total French herd and 5% of the European herd. Burgundy now has 450,000 milking cows of the Charolais race for 12,900 farms. The race is present in 73 of the French *départements* and in nearly 70 foreign countries. The carcasses have a high percentage of muscle and a low percentage of covering fat.

Nivernais - a genetic treasure exported throughout the world, as well as its succulent and marbled meat fattened in the pastures. These animals are the white blobs that one sees in the countryside: 1,400,000 heads! The same goes

for the chicken from Bresse, with its blue feet, white feathers and red crest, raised following strict traditional and natural methods on its patch of grass and grain. Anyone who has not enjoyed a capon from Bresse cannot even imagine the former pleasures of Byzance...

Blackcurrants, mustard and spiced bread

Several of "Burgundy's specialities" have acquired an international reputation. For example, the aniseed from Flavigny, the nougatine from Nevers. At Christmas in Dijon in the old days, the three kings brought the infant Jesus enough to please the whole family. Gold, frankincense and myrrh? What could he do with all that, the poor little baby in his cradle? No, here they brought blackcurrant liqueur for Mary, soft and sweet, without affectation, permeated with the fruit. Saint Joseph, somewhat hungry after all the emotion, was given a pot of mustard. Mustard strong and yellow, sharp enough to revive the dead, adding taste to anything lacking it. As for the Little One: spiced bread with a fine ribbon round it, a slab of health for teething when the

116

time comes. For the spiced bread from Dijon is very special. It is more like a rock than a sponge. But, how it melts in the mouth!

Many brotherhoods exist dedicated either to the snail, so dear to the writer Henri Vincenot, or the onion, or the *cacou* (non-stoned black cherries in a batter, a speciality of Paray-le-Monial). Each year, at the Dijon International Gastronomic Fair, the headquarters of French gastronomy organize special meetings. For example, the CNRS, the National Centre for Scientific Research, has created the European Centre for Taste Sciences in Dijon, to develop the research axes which are already well established (particularly for aromas).

A Burgundian menu

In Burgundy, a traditional meal begins with the aperitif, accompanied by golden and warm cheese cakes. Then, to begin with, a dozen snails cooked in a hundred different ways, jellied ham with chopped parsley, or eggs en meurette cooked gently in red wine. On the fish side, in the Saône Valley there is the *pauchouse*, a Burgundy fish casserole mixing carp, tench and pike, and all cooked with wine and onions.

On the meat side there is Burgundy *Potée* (cabbage and carrots boiled slowly with ham and pork), Boeuf Bourgignon (beef stewed in red wine), Piron saddle of hare, ham from Nuitonne (with wine), ham with cream or spicy sauce from Saulieu and, from Montberdois, *Coq au Vin*. The *andouillette*, a sausage made from chitterlings (from Chablis, Clamercy, Mâconnais) is greatly appreciated here.

Burgundy can also offer a fine cheese platter: the abbeys of Cîteaux and La Pierre-qui-Vire are splendid examples of this ancient monastic tradition. Epoisses and variations on it (Ami du Chambertin), Soumaintrain, cindered Aisy etc. There are excellent goat cheeses, particularly in the Mâconnais (Chèvreton, Bouton de culotte).

For dessert there will perhaps be a blackcurrant *vacherin* (made with meringue and cream) or a pear Belle Dijonnaise. And then, as digestive, a *marc* or a Burgundy brandy, or sloe gin. Burgundy uses blackcurrants, mustard and spiced bread in its cooking, to enhance the flavours of its produce. The cuisine is very inventive and the traditional recipe book is always being extended.

Flat bacon sausage and grated potatoes.
Photo Didier Benaouda.

European Institute of Taste Sciences and Nutritional Behaviour, in Dijon.
Photo D.R.

A sky full of stars

In Burgundy, gourmandise is not a sin. The first cookery books published in France date back to the XVIIth century and were the work of La Varenne, chef to the Marquis of Blé d'Uxelles in the Château of Cormatin. We owe him the famous *à la duxelles* preparation. Jean-Nicolas Margnery created a famous restaurant in Paris in the XIXth century and left his name to the Sole Margnery recipe. "Mother" Poulard invented the omelette of Mont-Saint-Michel, which has such a reputation; she top came from Burgundy, like the greatest chefs of yesteryear (Alexandre Dumaine, Fernand Point) and of today (Jean and Jacques Lameloise, Michel and Jean-Michel Lorain, Marc Meneau, Pierre Troisgros, Bernard Loiseau). Georges Blanc in Bresse also admits to being a Burgundian. The local sky is peopled with stars in all the good-food guides.

Where does kir come from?

Every single restaurant menu offers a kir or a royal kir. What an adventure! Canon Félix Kir (1876-1968) was elected mayor of Dijon for the first time at the age of 69, and stayed in the same post for twenty-three years. He willingly offered his guests an elixir composed of one third Dijon Cream of Blackcurrant and two-thirds Aligoté, a dry white wine as fresh as a spring breeze. Two products from the Hautes-Côtes, harmonising their contrasts. Since Canon Kir had a name simple to pronounce and easy to remember, it became a habit to call the aperitif "a kir". No doubt it existed before and he himself didn't actually invent it. But it still needed a name... And then there is the Kir royal, where the bubbly Crémant de Bourgogne replaces the Aligoté wine.

The Burgundy snail,
or *Helix pomatia*, incarnates the soul
of this land and the spirit of its
people. It can be found in stone,
either fossilized or sculpted in
Romanesque art (the church of
Saint-Seine-l'Abbaye),
or in Flamboyant Gothic
(Hôtel Chambellan in Dijon).
Henri Vincenot turned it
into a character in a novel.
Sleeper or traveller,
open or closed, grilled with salt,
prepared in
a thousand ways, it is open to all
suggestions. Like the tortoise in
Aesop's fable, it carries on its way
and faster than one thinks.
It is happy in its shell.
If you upset it, you will get nothing
out of it. If you win its confidence,
it will be faithful.
The spiral of its shell evokes
the universality of Burgundy itself.

The Charolais Herd Book

Since the end of the XIXth century,
the Herd Book,
or Pedigree Book has selected
the thoroughbred animals and listed
them according to their origins.
This keeps the race pure,
improves it through selection,
and defines
its criteria. It groups together
the animals whose ancestors have
been listed for at least
three generations.
Their performances and qualifications
are also recorded.
Since 1920, this register includes only
those animals whose parents were
already in the book.
The Herd Book, set up in Nevers,
promotes the Charolais race,
contacting breeders in the four corners of France and abroad.
There were 105,000 cows
inscribed in it in 1995,
out of a total
of 1.7 million in France.

Visits

◈ Arnay-le-Duc (Côte-d'Or) ◈
House of the Arts of the Table in the former Saint-Pierre Hospice, which presents a splendid exhibition on a gourmet theme each year.

◈ Auxerre (Yonne) ◈
Leblanc-Duvernoy museum and its faiences.
Charolles (Saône-et-Loire): traditional faiences (the "Charolles blue") and promotion of the Charolais race of cattle.

◈ Dijon ◈
Museum of Burgundian Life; The Mustard Museum created by Amora; the market (Tuesday and Friday); Annual International and Gastronomic Fair (end of October, beginning of November).

◈ Glux-en-Glenne (Nièvre) ◈
August, bilberry festival.

◈ Longchamp (Côte-d'Or) ◈
Shrine of the arts of the table.

◈ Louhans (Saône-et-Loire) ◈
Poultry market on Mondays, plus fairs.

◈ Mâcon (Saône-et-Loire) ◈
National festival of French wines in May.

◈ Magny-Cours (Nièvre) ◈
Promotion of the Charolais race.

◈ Marcigny (Saône-et-Loire) ◈
Goose and turkey festival, the second Monday in December.

◈ Moulins-Engilbert (Nièvre) ◈
Cattle market Mondays and Tuesdays.

◈ Nevers (Nièvre) ◈
Frédéric-Blandin museum and his Nevers faiences (the "Nevers" blue).

◈ Pierre-de-Bresse (Saône-et-Loire) ◈
Ecomuseum.

◈ Pouilly-sur-Loire (Nièvre) ◈
Wine festival in August.

◈ Reulle-Vergy (Côte-d'Or) ◈
Museum of Arts and Traditions of the Hautes-Côtes.

◈ Romenay (Saône-et-Loire) ◈
Rural and Poultry Museum.

◈ Saint-Christophe-en-Brionnais (Saône-et-Loire) ◈
Cattle market (Thursday mornings, early).

◈ Saulieu (Côte-d'Or) ◈
Spring each year, Gourmet Days, museum; Charolais days in August.

◈ Tournus (Saône-et-Loire) ◈
Perrin-de-Puycousin museum
(popular arts and traditions of the Tournugeois, Mâconnais and Bresse).

◈ Verdun-sur-le-Doubs (Saône-et-Loire) ◈
Wheat and Bread Centre.

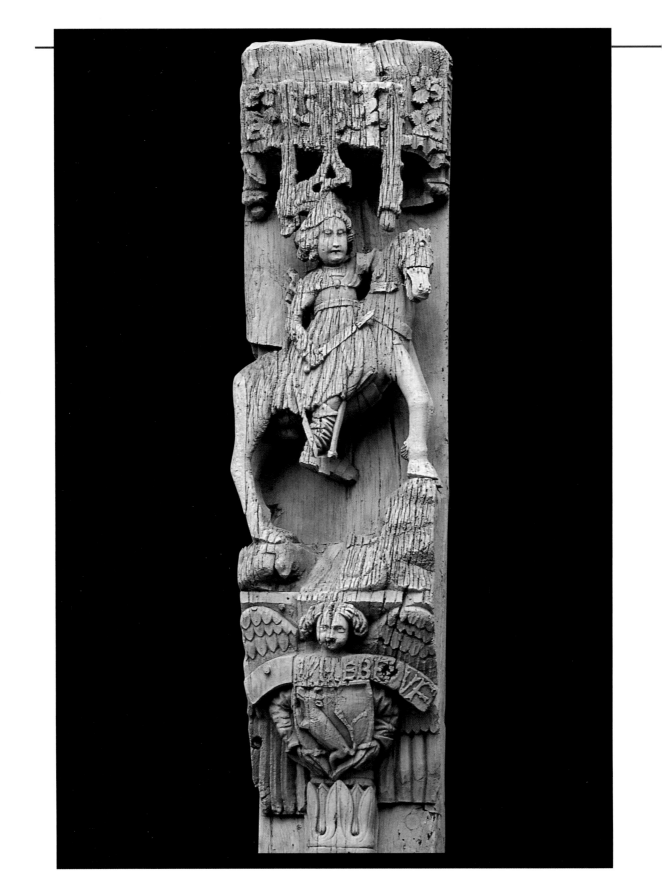

DATES TO REMEMBER

-500,000 B.C. ◆	First traces of the presence of man in Burgundy
- 300,000 B.C. ◆	Remains of a camp near Sens
- 60,000 B.C. ◆	Genay Man (Auxois)
- 20,000 B.C. ◆	Solutré Men
- 3,000 B.C. ◆	Chasséen Men
- 575 B.C ◆	The Vix Tomb
- 120 B.C ◆	Bibracte capital of the Eduens (Mont-Beuvray)
- 52 B.C. ◆	Vercingetorix conquered by Julius Caesar in Alésia
- 12 B.C. ◆	Augustodunum (Autun) founded, replaced Bibracte
21 A.D. ◆	Sacrovir uprising
312 ◆	Eumaeus Panegyric: the first economic description of the Beaune and Saône country.
477 ◆	The Burgondes take Dijon: birth of their kingdom, Burgondie.
534 ◆	The Burgonde kingdom conquered by the Francs.
841 ◆	Battle of Fontenoy-en-Puisaye, the parting of Charlemagne's Empire.
868 ◆	Foundation of Vézelay
888 ◆	Richard the Justiciary, Duke of Burgundy
909 ◆	Fondation of Cluny
936 ◆	Hugues, Grand Duke of Burgundy
1032 ◆	Robert I the Old, first Capetian Duke of Burgundy
1098 ◆	Fondation of Cîteaux
1315 ◆	Burgundian Charter
1364 ◆	Philip the Bold becomes Duke of Burgundy after the death of Philippe de Rouvres, last Capetian Duke of Burgundy: the Valois Dukes

1419	◆	Murder of John the Fearless - Philip the Good succeeds him
1430	◆	Foundation of the Order of the Golden Fleece
1467	◆	Charles the Bold succeeds Philip the Good
1477	◆	Death of Charles the Bold at the Battle of Nancy
1595	◆	Burgundy submits to Henry IV
1723	◆	Creation of the University of Dijon
1740	◆	Birth of the Academy of Sciences, Arts and Letters in Dijon
1789	◆	Taking of Dijon Castle
1832	◆	The Burgundy Canal opened, started in 1784
1934	◆	Creation of the Brotherhood of the Tastevin Knights
1941	◆	First regional Préfecture in Dijon.
1943	◆	Creation of the Regional Commissariat of the Republic of Burgundy and Franche-Comté in Dijon
1960	◆	Creation of the "Regional Programme" of Burgundy
1970	◆	Creation of the Regional Nature Park of the Morvan
1974	◆	The Regional Council and the Economic and Social Council of Burgundy
1986	◆	The Region of Burgundy becomes a territorial Collectivity, its members elected by universal franchise

Alésia, ... 6, 13
Alise-Sainte-Reine 25
Amognes 19
Ancy-le-Franc 62
Anost (forest) 18
Anzy-le-Duc 40
Arcy-sur-Cure 21
Armançon (river) 19
Arnay (country) 13
Arnay-le-Duc 18, 40, 121
Autun 14, 19
Auxerre 19
Auxerrois (region) 16
Avallon 19, 40, 85
Avallonnais (region) 16
Azé (caves) 71

Bailly 111
Lower Burgundy 8
Bazoches 62
Bazois 19
Beaujolais (region) 18
Beaune 51
Berzé-la-Ville 40
Bèze 19
Bibracte 6
Blanot 26
Blanzy 82
Blanzy (basin) 70
Boulaye (La) 36
Bourbince (La) 14
Bourbon-Lancy 40, 63
Bouzeron 104
Brancion 19, 40, 62
Bresse of Louhans (region) .. 19
Brionnais (region) 14
Bussière-sur-Ouche (La) 41

Chablis 101
Chablisien (region) 16
Chailley 82
Chailly-sur-Armançon 62
Chalon-sur-Saône 26, 73
Chamboux (lake) 18
Chapaize 40

Charité-sur-Loire (La) 42
Charolais (region) 14
Charolles 62
Chassey-le-Camp 26
Château-Chinon 11
Châteauneuf-en-Auxois ...13, 51
Châtillon-sur-Seine 17
Châtillonnais (region) 17
Chaumeçon (lake) 11
Chenôve 51, 77
Chitry-les-Mines 85
Cîteaux 6, 35
Clamecy 12
Clos-Vougeot 105
Cluny 6, 19
Commarin 63
Cormatin 63
Corton 101
Cosne-sur-Loire 40
Côte chalonnaise 17
Côte de Beaune 17
Côte de Nuits 17
Côte-d'Or 8
Couches 62
Creusot (Le) 59, 73
Cuiseaux 111

Decize 19
Dheune (river) 14
Dijon 87
Dijonnais (region) 17
Dompierre-les-Ormes 63
Donziais 19
Dun-les-Places 77

Epinac (basin) 70
Époisses 62

Fain-les-Moutiers 37
Ferté (La) 42
Fixin 73
Flavigny 116
Flavigny-sur-Ozerain 13, 40
Fleurie 101

Fontenay 41, 63
Fourchambault 77

Gâtinais (region) 12
Germolles 51
Gilly-lès-Cîteaux 41
Grosne (valley) 40

Haut Folin
(or Bois du Roi) 11
Upper Burgundy 8
Hautes-Côtes 18

Ignon (river) 17
Irancy 60, 104

Joigny 16, 62
Jovinien (region) 16

Langres (plateau) 16
Laroche-Migennes 77
Loire (river) 19
Longchamp 121
Louhans 121

Machine (La) 73
Mâcon 42
Mâconnais (region) 18
Magny-Cours 84
Marigny-le-Cahouët 85
Maulnes 62
Meursault 85
Mont-Saint-Jean 62
Montbard 17, 37
Montceau-l'Etoile 43
Montceau-les-Mines 73
Montcoy 63
Montjeu 63
Montrachet 101
Montréal 62
Morey-Saint-Denis 63
Morvan (region) 6

Moulin-à-Vent 101
Moulins-Engilbert 121

Nevers 43
Nièvre (département) 9
Nivernais (region) 14
Nuits-Saint-Georges 28

Othe (country) 11
Ouche (river) 18

Pannecière (lake) 11
Paray-le-Monial 6, 63
Pierre-de-Bresse 19, 63
Pierre-qui-Vire (La) 36
Pierreclos 62
Pommard 54
Pontigny 43
Pouilly-sur-Loire 19, 111
Prémeaux-Prissey 63
Puisaye 12

Quarré-les-Tombes 42

Reulle-Vergy 121
Revermont 19
Rochepot (La) 51
Romanèche-Thorins 111
Romanée-Conti 101
Romenay 121

Saint-Amand-en-Puisaye 12
Saint-Amour 101
Saint-Bris 104
Saint-Bris-le-Vineux 111
Saint-Brisson 11, 63
Saint-Christophe-
en-Brionnais 121
Saint-Fargeau 62, 63
Saint-Honoré-les-Bains ... 63, 85
Saint-Léger-Vauban 43
Saint-Loup-de-Varennes ... 70, 85

Saint-Martin-de-la-Mer 18
Saint-Sauveur-en Puisaye 12
Saint-Seine-l'Abbaye 32
Sainte-Colombe 70
Sancerrois (region) 19
Saône (river) 19
Saône-et-Loire 8
Saulieu 43, 121
Savigny-lès-Beaune 63
Semur-en-Auxois 13, 19
Semur-en-Brionnais 43, 62
Sénonais (region) 11
Sens 21
Serein (river) 18
Settons (Les) (lake) 11
Seurre 19
Sologne bourbonnaise (region) .. 19
Solutré 19
Sully 62, 73

Taizé 37
Talant 51
Tanlay 62

Thil 13
Tille (river) 17
Tonnerrois (region) 16
Toucy 62
Toulon-sur-Arroux 38
Tournugeois (region) 18
Tournus 18
Tracy-sur-Loire 85

Val des Choues 36
Val-de-Saône 18
Varzy 36
Vauluisant 43
Venelle (river) 17
Verdun-sur-le-Doubs 85, 121
Vergisson 19, 21
Vergy 62
Vingeanne (region) 17
Vix 21
Volnay 54

Yonne *(département)* 9

We would like to thank

The Dijon Fine Arts Museum
The Dijon Museum of Burgundy Life
The Beaune Wine Museum
The Dijon Municipal Library

Outside front cover: Vergisson (Saône-et-Loire).
Inset: the Nivernais canal near Coulanges-lès-Nevers (Nièvre) ;
the Fontenay Abbey cloister (Côte-d'Or).
Outside back cover: the Meursault cellars (Côte-d'Or); regional products. Photo D.R.

Cet ouvrage a été imprimé par Pollina S.A. 85400 Luçon - n° 71921A

ISBN 2 7373 2224.3 - Dépôt légal : mai 1997 - N° d'éditeur : 3612.01.03.05.97